Wealth of the World

EWAN BRADLEE LILLICII

ISBN 978-1-5483-7978-0   US$13.78
5 1 3 7 8 >

9 781548 379780

26 JUNE 2017

LMNTREE EDITION

With Love Across the Sea For
Harriet Ella Wheeler
The Romantic Reason
Besting My Best
Intention

Thanks to
Silence Dogood
Tammy Strickland
Thomas Joy
Many More

Inspired by
Pope Francis

With Appreciation to
Donald John Trump
Barack Hussein Obama
Vladimir Vladimirovich Putin
Emmanuel J-M Frederic Macron
Amateur Royal Families Everywhere

Based On Ideas Which Sprang Up
In Love With Kelly Yvonne Zuniga
December 13, 2013
Both Sides of Midnight

Wealth of the World

Contents

SECTION I
The Meaning That We Mind

Circling La Grange
Two Dollars Some Loosened Change
At Home On The Range

PREFACE
Flowers In The Desert

Figure 1Ourobouros. The dragon eating her tail.

CYCLICALITIES

Think of images you have seen or stories you may have heard depicting an ouroborus – a dragon (or serpent) eating her tail. This image represents the futile nature of cyclicality.

Imagine what a real such animal represents as she attempts this situation of bodily injury to avoid the struggle of poverty. From the perspective of the dragon's eyes, she has shielded herself from the harmful world with her armor as she spins in the abundance of her meal without argument. No matter how fast or how slow the beast eats she cannot discern the fact that her food will one day run out.

From the perspective of someone watching this ordeal take place a circumstance of certain decay toward the center is apparent. For a dragon that has become accustomed to the pain and focused on the comforting certainty of her hind part as breakfast it is impossible to recognize a bitter end in the making for lack of an horizon. Soon there is nothing left but the head no longer capable of taking a bite.

Figure 2Dwindling Cyclicality

From the perspective of movements over time this metaphor is one of cyclical degradation leading to immobility. Innovating mealtime by slipping out of the circle onto a new path of nutrition is essential to continuing existence. Sticking around without sticking her head up now and then is a certain safety safe for no one.

What might the beautiful creature do at the point of awareness to its predicament? She may consider how to maintain herself when the means of doing reemerges. If hope emerges while there is length left lingering subtle confidence may focus the dragon on an intention to avoid eating her tail again if only somebody, someone or something will save her life this time.

Self-awareness of the dragon's own locomotive power under comfortable control of a flawed course of action results in a path of negative progress toward a point of ultimate clarification. The dragon faces death as a result of avoiding the movements of life. From the outside looking in the dragon is an avatar of truthful conclusions from which the world around her may learn to avoid its own demise in direct or metaphorical terms if the outside observers maintain their wider perspective on the dragon's narrowing contributions to truth of existence. As the dragon draws closer to the end she becomes less a role model and more a caution to her own tail. To understand the difference, we simply make eye contact. To make a difference we write it down. To create a deference, we do something.

The one truth of conscious existence is progress. A progress path drawn over time resembles an arc with an upward slant. Awareness of that arc becomes obscured if the perspective of time in an individual consciousness is diminished. Drawing an arc repeatedly over a smaller perspective of time in negative circumstances - such as a dragon with nothing to eat - is harmful to a continuing awareness of progress. From the short-term perspective of a conscious being on a fearful, traumatic or lacking path life in our world may appear counter to a notion of progress or in direct opposition to notions of hope, faith or trust that our society is making progress.

Figure 3Progressive Cyclicality

Over time, many of those on a descending arc – such as the hungry serpent - are unable to see that fact until it is too late. From the perspective of the curious world indifferent to her death the dragon remains an avatar of truthful conclusiveness. Those of the dragon's friends watching nearby who have balanced their cyclicality into being consider what to do next.

As she harms herself in apparent bliss she invites the others to share short-term dwindling perspective. This provides the dragon momentary hope by projection while offering a path of seeming complement; yet denies the joy possible from recoiling into a spring of faith leading to renewed trust inspiring the world around the dragon to be a more trustworthy place to live.

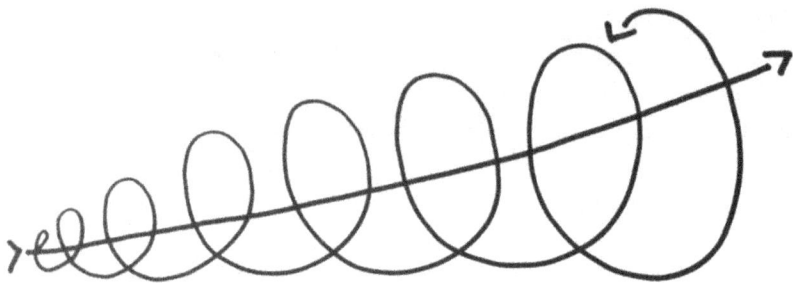

Figure 4Progress Arc

Life arrives, blossoms and makes choices while within the compassionate hand basket of the increasing life of its environment. Living a life of progress that identifies, supports and reacts positively to the lives making progress around it is a perpetual learning and teaching experience periodically requiring the act of doing so that it may continue to follow an arc. Over time, an upwards arc sets no maximum boundary for those acting with sincerity along it. A never-ending story – conclusively.

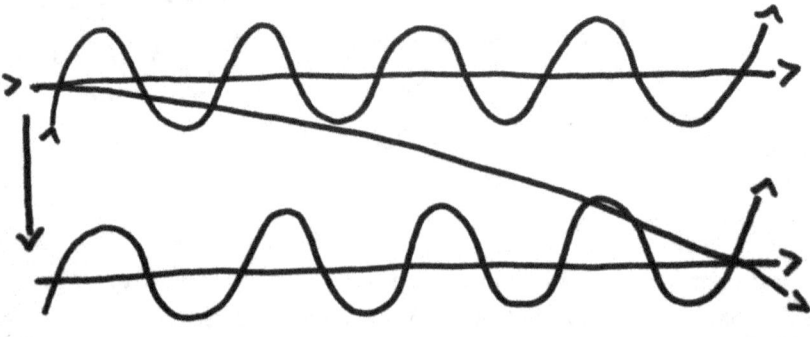

Figure 5Progressive Cycles maintain the feeling of progress while lowering the mean over

time.

Choice of a path opposed to your life's improvements, your meaningful progress or to force flawed lines of progressive and dwindling cyclicality upon another being that does you no harm is the opposite of good for anyone aware of doing so. In the metaphor of political power, for instance, when a society's leadership seeks to control the behavior of citizens they have been elected to lead on an arc of progress such a leadership will erode the power of the people who lent it to them by election.

In time, if subsequent leaderships follow a predecessor's role model of control the arc will become burdened by a cyclicality diminishing the power held by the offices of leadership and validate a dwindling tradition for all citizens of the society to follow. The clarifying event is already available to understand for awareness wherever a dictatorship on Earth has fallen to leave the perpetrator powerlessly hoping that perfection of control will lead to renewed salvation. If a dwindling cyclicality could lead a world to positive progress it would have happened by now. Balanced cycles of limited progress riding a flat line lower the mean slowly over perspectives of time hiding a downward arc from identification.

Figure 6Strategies wipe out. Plans sail against the waves. Master plans soar into the air.

Instead, let us vindicate the dragon with the potential in its own head. What does cyclicality of an improving, progressive nature look like? I suggest it looks like wiggles and squirms in every possible direction toward any goal this beautiful being chooses so long as it is not the place from where she came. With her back to the start, a serpent blooms in a sense – outward from herself. Over a reasonable amount of time that blooming growth from within is indicated by girth, the shedding of skin and the lengthening of her tail.

The ouroborus is meaningful as a metaphor to understand cyclicality of a mathematical nature. An astute mathematician could determine for you the time left in the descent to a mere head, for instance, by observing from an outside perspective complementary to math and applying geometric calculation structures that have been proven certain to organize numerical details of time.

Providing certainty of outcome through structural integrity on a descending path of diminishing sight and progress, however, becomes its own short-sightedness as the focus of awareness builds faith without doing that which may inspire belief – offering help to the dragon. Lack of understanding life may renew or redeem itself provides no good role model, no good learning experience and no good basis to educate for anyone momentarily comforted by the cold certainty of a downward arc. A sinking ship must seal its sieve to reemerge or face a clarifying submergence.

I suggest a person that makes progress as a biology, or a society of people that aspire to the competencies of improving biological beings, would be wiser to follow a more practical biological metaphor. The certainty of mathematics cannot be applied to the certain mystery of blooming growth from within. There is no way to gain perspective from the outside that moves beyond faith and momentary certainty of cyclicality that feels like a knowing faith without sharing the wisdom gained from witnessing the outcomes of ones blossoming growth to seed those around living lives on their own complementary path, as they all blossom together.

Let's apply this to a society as large as the United States of America and its progress.

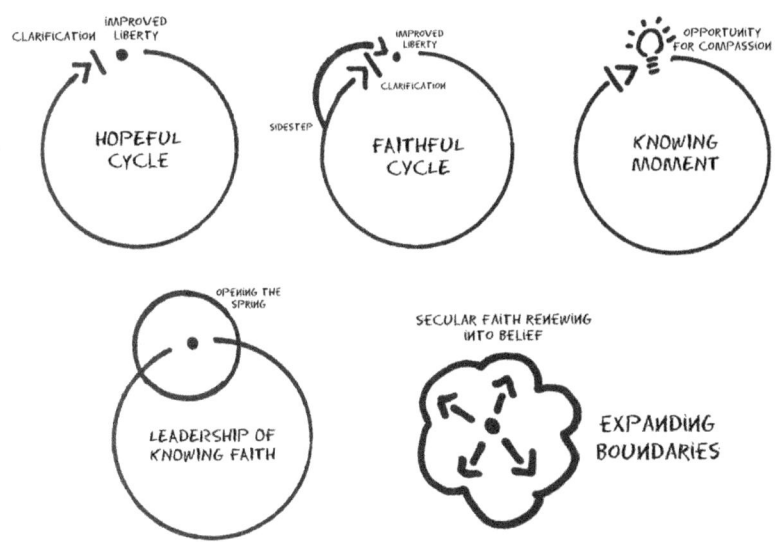

FROM GEOMETRIC TO BIOLOGICAL METAPHOR

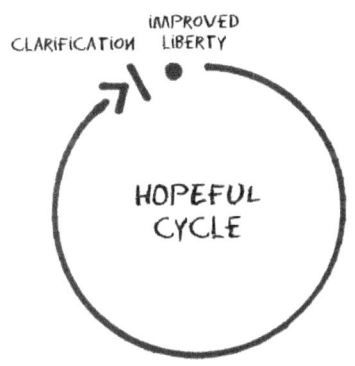

Hopeful Cycle

Consider the dwindling cyclicality of negative societal progress. Much like the ouroborus, this circular path leads a society towards a clarifying moment of truth. When this path is taken by an individual the clarification may become one without the means to recover. In a society of hundreds of millions of people, if the primary metaphor of renewal for the sake of progress is allowed to be one of dwindling cyclicality or the flat balance of progressive cyclicality it can be a detriment to the individuals learning from such role models.

Progressive cycles balance on two axis while diminishing sight on the third follows lowering of the mean or expanding perspective follows raising the mean. Without a guidebook, those riding this ark of faith depart in twos to find their own ways of understanding the awareness of the captain that brought them there. Dwindling cycles appear to speed up without acceleration as they move through time. From the perspective of those involved in role modeling and following the conclusions of a perfecting cycle of harm these understandings appear to be valuable as they increase in relative proximity. Any notion of awareness gained or progress being made is an illusion based on the diminishing time perspectives of those within the learning experience and those on the outside being trained by the only observable lessons. From a longer view the understandings gained are mere momentarily comforting certainties building fewer foundations for a dwindling set of choices fitting within them.

> *Student*: *"How do we improve?"*
>
> *Teacher*: *"Good choices."*
>
> *Student*: *"How do we understand a good choice?"*
>
> *Teacher*: *"Experience."*
>
> *Student*: *"How do we gain experience? Bad choices?"*
>
> *Teacher*: *"Successful mistakes. Consider your involvement from the other end of the chosen way. Clear that path with determination, sincerity and intention as your guides."*

Traumas are poor learning experiences for those within them and anything but teaching experiences for those on the outside of them offering indifference to those inside. In a society of billions of people, cyclical trauma is luckily overcome in large numbers when viewed as a segment of population. Yet the comfort of that mathematical certainty obscures both the feelings of ongoing harm in the individuals that do not reemerge and the growing feeling of uncertain life ahead in the people that do reemerge to the certainty of a new submergence without a life raft over and over again.

The human allusion to the arriving clarification point and its subsequent point of improved liberty is a sense of emotional distress over a harm in the being or in the making followed by the removal of that harm and happier feelings. When the clarification is overcome arrival at an improved liberty is achieved momentarily.

Whether it will be a permanent progress or return as a harm that builds an awareness of itself is up to the sight of those on the path and the faith they have in those that give them their interpretation from somewhere off the path.

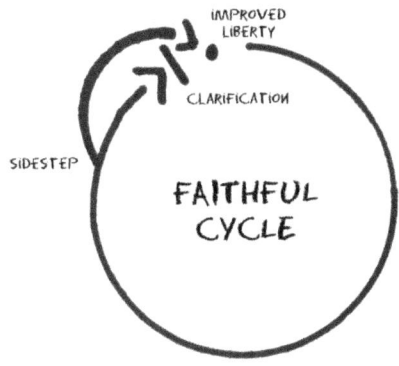

Faithful Cycle

In the next cycle, wisdom that respects its own perspectives and the perspective of sincere observers will lead to an understanding of detrimental circumstances reaching a tipping point within an improving society. The path of progress leads back up to the clarification built upon those detriments now understood in order to educate the participants in the society on the error of their ways. Those unaware or uninterested in this educational event are likely to slide into it on a reflective curve dimpling the circle. Avoidance of the clarifying event by side step with tipping point awareness eases you into an improved liberty without the negative aspects of a harsh lesson of clarification. In the United States, we are fortunate to have a multi-directional respect for perspectives built in to our system of governance to do just that.

Legislative, Executive and Judicial are three perspectives that make up the support structure of our principled Constitutional ideals. Our leaders, representatives and most ideal judges are the architectural reflection of our agreement to exist as a society. Our civil servants can sense the structure because they exist among it. They can view it from the outside looking toward it because their perspectives extend beyond the perimeter in the form of ambassadors to other nations, vertical communication from single citizen to state governor to president and back around and the wisdom of the past coupled with master plans for the future.

Yet when it comes to the interior that flows toward center their sight must give way to faith that the perspective of counterparts in state and local reflections of their own structure as well as the citizens themselves will be as sincere as their own. Sincerity alone can be the sole nature of a perspective seeking communication up, down and across this structure. When everyone involved in our society has faith in each other that communication overcomes clarifications, degradations of progress and flawed courses of action with ease.

A MOMENT OF FAITH

Knowing Moment

Once a society passes a clarifying event with awareness it is time to consider a more efficient means of improvement in avoidance of cyclical harm. Instead of circling around, stand on your improved liberty with compassion and begin to enlarge your Utopian boundary from that spot.

Leadership of Knowing Faith

Crystallize the inspiration, secular faith and optimism of the moment and perpetuate it with new agreements based on accumulated wisdoms from the circle that builds an enlarging sphere around your truth. When all major harms have been identified and it remains merely to enforce existing harms out of existence holding on to that moment of faith and putting it into motion achieves a march toward arrival at heaven on Earth led by a leader with knowing faith. A moment of faith in perpetual motion.

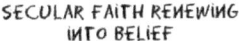

EXPANDING BOUNDARIES

Expanding Boundaries

A human society is literally a collection of biological beings making progress toward an ideal expression of the ideals upon which expressions are based. The ideal perfection and certainty of a circle to represent progress is misleading. Geometry is not fitting. A biological metaphor such as a flower is a more apropos reflection of the true architecture and path of that architecture across time. Decorate your society's moment of secular faith awareness with that flower. Let it bloom as time and your society move forward.

EVERY ISSUE FITS WITHIN IT AND EVERY FAITH THRIVES AMONG THEM.

Laying the many flowers of all Utopian Capitalist nations on top of each other becomes a flowering 3D representation of world progress. As they change throughout time with progress up and around they bloom into a beautiful 4th dimensional flower. Understanding the cause and effect underlying faith of every kind of citizen from a societal perspective leads toward understanding the nature of mind. Understanding the typical flow of events underlying moments of choice from every perspective out toward, and inward from, every other perspective are the building blocks of wisdom, compassion and awareness.

> **Pope Francis had this to say in regard to the effects of the current Capitalist philosophy:** *"The worship of the ancient golden calf has returned in a new and ruthless guise in the idolatry of money and the dictatorship of an impersonal economy lacking a truly human purpose. The worldwide crisis affecting finance and the economy lays bare their imbalances*

> *and, above all, their lack of real concern for human beings; man is reduced to one of his needs alone: consumption."*

Utopian Capitalism answers the call with a truly human purpose. What follows is the philosophical and practical understanding to support all necessary consumption on Earth without struggle – leaving every citizen free to decide when, how and what to create with their talent, contribute with their intentions and share with their compassion in a global society that shares its faith, abundance and compassion in kind with them.

SECTION II
The Deference That It Takes

Epic Hero Deeds
Love Poetry Wrote With Ease
July Fourth Proceeds

Ewan Lillicii

CHAPTER 1
Wealth of the World

UTOPIA + CAPITALISM

When Utopia and Capitalism have been considered in the past the tendency has been for one to modify the other. I suggest Utopia can exist as a complement to Capitalism that is completely unique. The moment you define Utopia with details you are limiting the perspective of someone else within it. The ideal of Utopia must be defined by structural components alone. Utopia is a perspective defined by boundaries inside of which everything is possible in every number of ways. In this way, it opposes chaos – an environment containing every detail and without boundary.

From a personal perspective, Utopia is our best life detailed within this boundary. Capitalism is the means by which we may all take ownership of our best life to make it last. As complements, they are a promise by society to support and improve an environment for citizens which helps them achieve their personal perspective on Utopia. As Utopia achieves a level of improvement in the lives of each citizen it will invigorate a new, purer and sustainable Capitalism reinforcing the strength of integrated social improvements.

Outdated methods of behavior control/limitation will be replaced with behavior improvement opportunities, inspirations and environments. To live and thrive in an improved society is to complement that society with your own improvements – more responsible, more thoughtful, more well-planned people. This doesn't happen overnight. But the motivation to do so is the strongest on Earth. Money.

Utopian Capitalist societies will pay every citizen of working age the same regionally-adjusted amount to support an average Struggle-free Life.

Unlike behavior limitation, improvement opportunities are primarily self-directed and cannot be enforced. They must be inspired by environment under direction of the individual while being guided by the environment society provides for such progress to take place. Better metaphors, such as Struggle-free Life itself, and the environment in which similar ways of life can be achieved and supported as they thrive must be made apparent. The combination of education, motivation and awareness will then occur naturally. The evidence is wealthy people. Once they achieve a Struggle-free Life they do not typically end their motivated lives of improvement. Neither will the poor and middle-class whose struggles are alleviated.

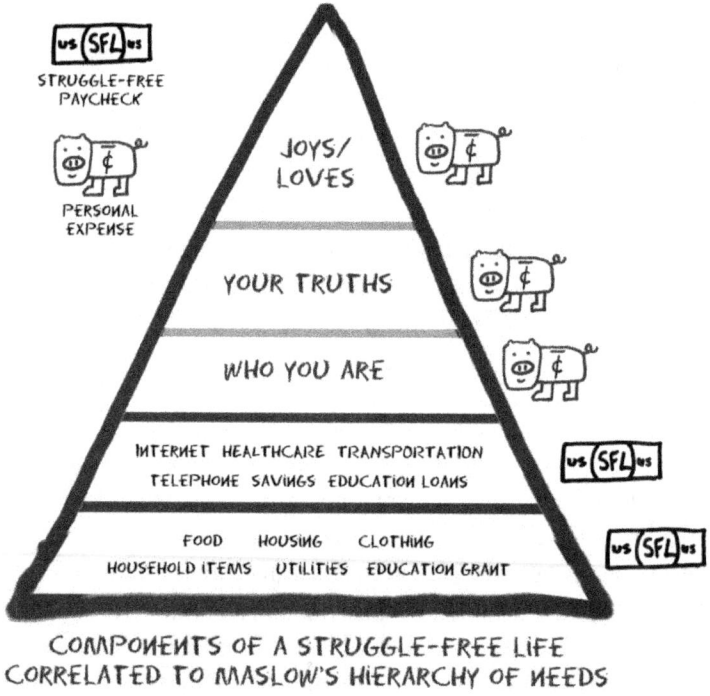

COMPONENTS OF A STRUGGLE-FREE LIFE
CORRELATED TO MASLOW'S HIERARCHY OF NEEDS

Sending every adult citizen, the money it takes to step up the bottom two rungs of the Maslow's Hierarchy of Needs is at once the means and the inspiration to end cyclical struggle in favor of purposeful challenges on a path toward long-term goals and achievements. Once struggle is removed from life's equation citizens are free to focus upon their own responsible guidance, their paths to joy and their meaningful expressions of that joy inspiring others to their own unique experiences and contributions to society. These ends are achieved the way democratic Capitalists achieve these results – with respect for choice, private ownership and assistance in the form of currency.

This is a rare opportunity to show concern and compassion from the top of our society all the way to an individual at the base. For a single citizen, and every citizen, to feel the care of their society inspires faith and fosters trust in time. Utopian Capitalism makes this rare opportunity a monthly occurrence. Secular faith in motion.

The confidence and faith to plan a life inclusive of challenges building up to long-term achievements comes from men and women assisted to break free of cyclical struggle and the ongoing promise from their society that struggle will never be a reoccurring problem in their lives again. As their faith becomes trust over time it will reinforce the secular faith created by the moment of inspiration initiating Utopian Capitalism. The continuing compassion of Struggle-free Life and more truthful shared understandings of economics, Infinite Currency by Unanimous Consent and currency valuation standards are what it takes to earn that trust.

MODULARITY

The unique architecture of Utopian Capitalism is not only flexible, but modular as well. Modularity respects the intention of the original social agreement throughout time. As long as society benefits from an individual's ability to overcome struggle the Utopian Capitalism architecture will remain practical. In this way, the intention itself is maintained separate from the structure of its implementation.

Take a closer look at the modular components I suggest are relevant to the leadership of our country, the social benefits of implementing the philosophy which begin to materialize almost immediately and the notion of a modular means to achieving the intention and maintaining faith in the social agreement.

The act of compassion initiating Utopian Capitalism philosophy and Struggle-free Life, the means by which the leadership perspectives are supported and social benefits are achieved, the metaphorical innovation to geometric understandings and the modularity of the architecture itself are all inspirations that individually inform our society at a fundamental level that we intend to exist and improve as a nation for any foreseeable future. Together, they keep us collectively on a path of progress that our most sincere and brilliant founders, Presidents, representatives, justice officials and patriotic citizens can be proud of as they watch with pride as the angels on our shoulders.

GOVERNMENTAL PERSPECTIVES

Compassion from the Top

In 2017 America there is an opportunity for compassion to convey to every citizen individually that our leadership and the federal government itself has concern for them and an awareness of changing needs, human potential and the passive role of society in personal improvement. That opportunity increases with low participation brought on by disillusionment with war, under-representation within gerrymandered districts and narrowed perspectives focused upon issues of struggle. The inspiration potential increases as the notions that those in the 1% care about those in the 99% degrade.

The long-term value and perpetual support for our economy, quality of life and principled living are benefits of a perspective shift on the goals that skills and wealth we already possess can achieve in a short amount of time.

A significant harm in our society is financial savagery. Absence of money when it is vital to the ongoing happy lives we have achieved can create a misery when it happens cyclically. Unemployment, illness, caring for a family member, loss of investment value, unjust enforcement for the sake of regulation over circumstance and other situations prohibitive of your personal path to long-term goals are a collective harm as well as a personal tragedy.

Removal of harm from our environment is the fundamental job of society. It's why society comes together in the first place. When the harm of financial savagery is removed from our lives, it is a reminder that compassion can still come from the top of our society and be felt by the individual at the base.

Inspiration that Endures

Unlike moments of war threat or civil liberty achievement the benefits from a Struggle-free Life occur every month when the money to achieve them is received. The memory of this good deed is renewed twelve times per year -

every year. A moment of faith in perpetual motion.

Understanding Among Citizens

Uncertainty creates the first notions of stress surrounding money. Having a financial vehicle of certain, consistent value to place the stressful holdings of every other portion of your savings is how we can take the worry out of money. Lack of worry is a certainty inspiring faith, and ultimately trust, we will all understand as a basis for every other understanding between and among us.

Role Model to the World

Once the United States displays to the world that Utopian Capitalism has eliminated the poverty line it will be the viral metaphor of the next decade. As other nations use our template for Infinite Currency's structure they will spread Capitalism - and most likely a democratic spirit - across continents.

The necessary support to do so will exist in the ability to exchange domestic currencies with confidence and to value each nation with the same transparency as the leaders of these new secular faith-managed systems bring to their sincere leadership.

Projecting out the faithfulness of value in an individual's work and appreciation to the national level utilizes Bureau of Labor Statistics data to organize the work force by career. Combining this amount of Work Potential with the total value of societal resources is a meaningful way to create national value.

The World Bank, United Nations or other world body can then promote workforce details in support of a world-wide master plan guidance by assigning multipliers to specific career paths. When a nation is focused domestically they will not pay much attention to multipliers. However, when they are of an international perspective they will tend to follow incentives in order to achieve a higher total valuation for their country and its wealth.

Credit to the Government

In the United States our society provides its "beings" (humans and wildlife) with services such as a government, law enforcement, food benefits, etc. Planning for the environment in which we will achieve and investing in advance to prepare it is a common practice in our society.

What about the budget our government comes up with every year? Can they reasonably come up with new currency value out of thin air?

Yes. But it doesn't come from air. It comes from faith that if our society provides an environment where opportunities exist we will achieve in that environment. Therefore, an advance of credit is faithful.

When we deduct another unanimously agreed faithful expenditure – the cost of maintaining a struggle-free life – from the list of tax-based expenses in our government budget our nation will benefit in these ways:

- Trusting a government acting sincerely to inspire the population to progress and explaining its actions in comprehensive, plain-spoken truth makes all government expenditures faithful - no taxes required. While it may be decades before this occurs, considering the ideal of eliminating personal taxation is a reasonable thought.
- Reduction of the corporate tax to a level providing us with a Faithful Source of tax revenue to cover discretionary spending and elevation of correlated corporate taxation as a level of self-regulation against monopolies.
- Set a precedent for future expenditures funded by unanimous consent in which we allow our government to make on our behalf, such as foreign debt, requiring no taxation or reduction of government savings.

SOCIETAL BENEFITS

Eliminate Poverty

Struggle-free means we have all the money we need to buy all the food, household and personal care items we need. The war on poverty begun by President Johnson is over. We win!

Food benefits are great when you need them. Yet at just over $2 per meal they still require constant watch to avoid running out. Struggle-free is food and every other thing a person needs for the fundamentals of a life free to focus on long-term goals.

End of War

Once a nation begins to see the opportunities presented by a struggle-free population and begins to fill in its national personality with a long-term master-planning focus it will begin to create value that builds upon itself.

Who will want to risk their value being destroyed? War will become a much more distasteful alternative compared with conflict resolution even for those among us trained to see only two sides to every option. Our current military will decrease in size as those who entered into the armed forces for a steady paycheck will find that security elsewhere. Those who stay will become our next great explorers to places like the Moon, Mars, Antarctica and under the sea.

This is a big deal. Perhaps the biggest reward of them all. The end of war on Earth marks the first time nations on the whole will not suffer from cyclical struggle. Every national psychology is a reflection of the sum of each citizen's psychological part.

To have been the "world's policeman" even for a century at a time when every other facet of human life is getting more stressful takes a toll on your emotions – and on the group emotions of the United States.

Withdrawing from a world theater no longer interested in playing war and destruction will do us all – in the U.S. and the rest of the world – much good as we think on opportunities beyond our cyclical quagmires.

Economic Stability

Think back seven or so years ago when the European Union nations began to lose faith in their Euro currency and economies descended the public into chaos. Do you remember which two countries were notable for avoiding failure? Britain and the United States. Why?

Both countries share their currencies with other nations with more faith in the dollar and the pound than in their own currency. That cross-border faith keeps everyone afloat even when faith may falter in one or a few of the currency-sharing countries.

> ***Consider this:*** *Another aspect of economic buoyancy is the fact that when you project faith on the dollar or pound there is a place and a historical record of faith returned to associate with it. A faith projection unavailable in a Euro or a Bitcoin.*

Now imagine if every nation had their own national currency while sharing similar faith-supportive structure for keeping its value stabilized. Projections of faith would be placed upon the authors of such a structure and then in time on the structure of stability itself.

Knowing every nation in the world shares a stable structure is support for a major component of societal agreement using monetary means. That awareness shares faith which in turn lends an faithful economic hand when national personality is attacked by loss of faith in other facets of society. National currencies will suffer no more collapse. Anywhere.

No Personal Income Taxes

Taxes. Why bother?

Income details will still be submitted to the government by each American for analysis and statistical purposes. Government will fund itself from a percentage of the prior year's GDP set in advance by the three branches of our government with Infinite Currency by Unanimous Consent. States will operate the same way with a combination of corporate tax revenue and Infinite Currency. If there is ever a sincere need to go beyond the set limits a representative will draw up a proposal and submit it for approval. No community in America will ever go bankrupt again.

That doesn't mean the IRS has to lay off employees either. They do a great job of organizing, transferring and mailing out hundreds of millions of checks every year. We need their expertise to deliver struggle-free payments on time every time.

From a personal perspective, no taxes paid by any citizen means salaries will lessen, costs will go down for employers, innovation will be motivated to occur and the opportunity of available cash to risk corporate apprenticeships and other collaborative ventures with our faithful currency savings will ensure it does.

Affordable Care Premium

Health insurance, car insurance, and other forms of insurance deemed to be part of a Struggle-free Life will be accounted for within the struggle-free amount paid to every adult citizen. How much it costs will not be a concern. If premiums quadruple the cost will be OK. Every citizen will still be able to afford what we deem to be part of a Struggle-free Life.

Struggle-free means eating the kinds of foods right for your body. A gluten-free diet, for instance, can be very beneficial to your health if you are averse to gluten. It's also a very expensive diet to maintain. Struggle-free payments will take your dietary needs and other medically and health-appropriate necessities into account.

Employment Issues

When a person has the ability to sustain life without struggle above the bottom two tiers of the Maslow's Hierarchy of Needs they never lose sight of their goals and long-term plans. [1]

Problems such as a layoff or inability to find work in a double-digit unemployment environment are no longer situations of imminent destruction. These setbacks become mere delays during which time savings and intention remain intact.

20% unemployment? No problem. Except for one. What is your Congressman doing? He has all the money he needs! Does he know his district wants to get back to work? Help the city break ground on a new junior college fast. Seed another venture to innovate the hydrogen fuel industry and begin soliciting public funds to incentivize growth of the platform in ways others can pick up and run with.

We will achieve these ends with no public ownership. Seed capital and incentives requiring no payback when private funds are not available and master planning schedules are involved will be used as incentives to create open architecture platforms whenever possible in order to benefit the multiplication of opportunity. Stronger capitalism with sincere guidance.

Crime Reduction

Larceny, auto theft and burglary will see dramatic decreases in number of incidents when everyone is given the opportunity to have a Struggle-free Life. Crime in general is a result of people with their backs against the wall.

When the entire population realizes that it will never again face the kind of struggle which can destroy their goals or defeat their will to improve. That confidence will have an immediate effect on crime. Time perspectives will widen so that momentary feelings of lack will no longer overpower long-term goals

The role model of government concerned about each citizen at the individual level is a strong metaphor for compassion. Compassionate citizens will follow in kind – showing that compassion toward each other in increasing numbers.

Improved Patriotism

Imagine how people will feel about their country when expenditures of government become more transparent and plain-spoken, crime descends, the U.S. becomes a strong role model in the world again and everyone gets a struggle-free check as a token of the compassion we all have for each other and the value we give each other's work and artistry.

Immigration Issues

When other countries adopt our model for Utopian Capitalism it will be the end of negative immigration issues. Citizens of any struggle-free country will opt to stay in the place they grew up unless they have the intention to be a part of a foreign national personality – the kind of immigrants every nation desires!

When given the opportunity to build their nation the way they choose without struggles of joblessness weighing on their lives every citizen of every nation will likely stay and improve their part of the Earth.

Secular Faith Renewed

Religion and faith go hand in hand. Yet religion is just one means to achieving faith. When you consider the multi-directional trust and goodwill Americans have for each other it speaks to a different kind of faith – secular faith.

When a compassionate inspiration like struggle-free living is given to the entire nation at once by the government it looks like a graph entirely shaded in. A moment when everyone understands each other with the potential to last forever.

We are all at the mercy of financial savagery from time to time. Whether you are on welfare or have a billion dollars in the bank. Whether you are a city employee that must deal with budget shortfalls or a Congressman that must deal with periodic government shutdowns in the latter part of December. Everyone understands the harm of the struggle. Everyone will understand the solution promoting secular faith.

Perspectives Widen

People who struggle think less about their future and more about their present survival. Time perspective shrinkage is one reason people commit crime – they feel as though there is no other option or that only the current day matters and the long-term repercussions don't have to be considered. A shrinking sense of community perspective also contributes to social problems.

IF AT FIRST YOU DON'T SUCCEED WAIT AROUND UNTIL JUST AFTER YOUR LAST TRY.

When citizens begin to feel less separate from other groups in their local society their community perspectives will widen. They will intend their goals, plan how to achieve them and keep trying to achieve them through setbacks. There is no chain of events to follow there is only will. The more wills around an intention the more often intentions all ways will.

INTENTION IS ALWAYS WILL.

Focusing on upper levels of the Maslow's Hierarchy of Needs without ever falling below the bottom two rungs will widen time and community perspectives in each American. Those healed fractures will then complement each other for renewed growth in a new renaissance of apprenticeships with understandings of opportunity.

Opportunities Blossom

Once cyclical struggles are cleared from the national agenda our Executive and Legislative branches are free to think upon opportunity creation in partnership with the business, social and investment leaders of our country. After decades of cyclical issues taking up space in our political conversations many people may have a hard time considering what else there is to concern our government.

The answer is simple – everything else.

Foreign Policy

As the social ills of the world's first Utopian society begin to fall away and the understanding of limitless challenges rise to take the place of cyclical struggle other nations will find themselves anxious to duplicate our success.

STRATEGIES GUIDE ACTIONS TO POINTS. PLANS MOTIVATE STRATEGIES TO ACHIEVEMENTS. MASTER PLANS OF FUNDAMENTAL PRINCIPLE INSPIRE THEM ALL WITH COMPASSIONATE MEANINGFULNESS.

Foreign Policy will become Foreign Friendship as we assist those early adopters who implement our system using their own currency to achieve domestic stability, faith and prosperity. Countries that have been decimated by currency fluctuation and loss of faith will become our long-term friends with a well-deserved appreciation for our Struggle-free ideals.

Inclusive Thinking

Struggle-free is not the same as welfare. The fact that it will be paid to every American regardless of financial situation will eliminate the notion of some people taking advantage of what others contribute. As superior thinking fades its absence will assist in healing fractures of social strata that have contributed to misunderstandings among large groups of people within our nation. The kinds of misunderstandings that lead to racial violence, discrimination and indifference to suffering.

Even if a person chooses to never work again at the very least they will be viewed as a great customer with that 10% of surplus they can use to buy a new TV every year or go on a vacation.

In Utopian Capitalism the rich will get richer. Yet the poor will no longer be poor. They will be secure. There will be more opportunities to become wealthy and achieving financial independence will be a more realistic goal for those that desire it.

COMPETITION REPLACES YOUR GOALS WITH THE GOALS OF YOUR FELLOW COMPETITORS.

To merely achieve the plateau of being rich above the poor is an inferior thought to becoming as wealthy as you intend. To achieve it means allowing for everyone else along for the ride who wants to be there.

Heroes, Legends & Justice

New legends are a suitable addition to history as we start the new calendar Age of Aquarius. The President, his Vice-President and his White House that initiate a struggle-free Utopian Capitalism will be legends for the next thousand years.

Members of Congress will be heroes in their home districts. Citizens will feel part of a special moment in time. There is much inspiration to go around.

When faith of an individual is considered the foundation of national wealth we literally can't do it without YOU.

Benefit of Having Enough: Master-planning Our Nation

WITH THE MONEY TO MOTIVATE THE WILL TO FOLLOW INTENTIONAL PROGRESS YOU CAN MASTER PLAN YOUR WAY INTO ANY FUTURE.

In our lifetimes, the United States government has followed a metaphor of reaction to clarification that fits its personality as projected onto it by the rest of the world. We have been the world's policeman. Just like our military, policemen do not react until a harm has been committed or is imminent. In the reflection of society's willingness to act to avoid harm to the civilian population, however, restraint is not a virtue since judgment of an equitable harm is unnecessary.

HISTORY REPEATS ITS MISTAKES AND MAINTAINS ITS SUCCESSES.

Instead, principled action is the stronger persuasive argument to alleviate common threats to life or its quality. Once threats are alleviated and opportunity creation becomes the focus to sustain a matching reflection in Behavior Improvement the notions of restraint or allowance are replaced by notions of better directions on the shared path of your master plan.

Innovation Incentives

Innovations that support our future intention for growth or create a platform for others to create their artistry upon may be offered incentives by the government in the form of: (1) Priority to mentor new companies/industries the government helps fund with a cut of the profit as they mature (2) Cash incentives (3) Organizational real estate (4) Voice in planning matters related to the new industry

It's important to realize that this is NOT socialism. These are incentives given by the government to jump-start industries part of a master plan so that the timing of that plan will continue to be accurate.

When incentives support the population with interesting careers and more opportunity there is no problem – especially when they become so commonplace that they are no longer seen as being unfair. Thank you, USA.

Representation Returns

PLANS INCLUDE YOUR PEOPLE. MASTER PLANS INCLUDE ALL YOUR PEOPLE.

When our Congress is allowed to fund every good detail it can think up for each Congressman's, Congresswoman's and Senator's district and state along a master-planning structure a few things will happen. Exceptional things.

535 Congressmen and Congresswomen will have the potential to become heroes in their district every year. Gerrymandering will heal itself as representatives will desire to take advantage of the money multiplier to enrich their districts without flowing over the boundaries into another district

Steady streams of solutions to rising problems will emerge and cyclical problems will be solved once and for all.

Literacy

More opportunities will foster an environment of desire for education and self-improvement. All of which is built on a foundation of literacy. Environments of depression, struggle and disconnected citizens that once fostered illiteracy will be virtually eliminated. The ability to thrive without fear of what the future may bring will replace those situations with optimism and motivated learning.

Higher Education

Infinite Currency allows our society to fund the situations it needs on time all the time. When under-served career paths are part of our long-term plan they can be incentivized with full-tuition scholarships for new students or those changing careers.

Social Security / Retirees

The fear of an underfunded Social Security System is no longer an issue. Retirees will receive the same struggle-free paycheck as all adults. Along with their savings, that makes retirement more of an ease and joy. It also leaves retirement age up to the individual without thought to any penalties from the Social Security System.

Family Neighborhoods

Return to family values in a neighborhood is a function of mobility and decreased necessity to move for economic reasons. Values and the good feelings of neighbors who are friendly and interact in neighborly ways are durable and will return to urban neighborhoods when the need to move from a home in order to extract the equity or to avoid a personal financial collapse are mitigated with Struggle-free Life payments which will guide them past the struggles of cyclical unemployment and other current economic reasons for moving households several times during an adult lifetime.

A MOMENT OF FAITH IN PERPETUAL MOTION

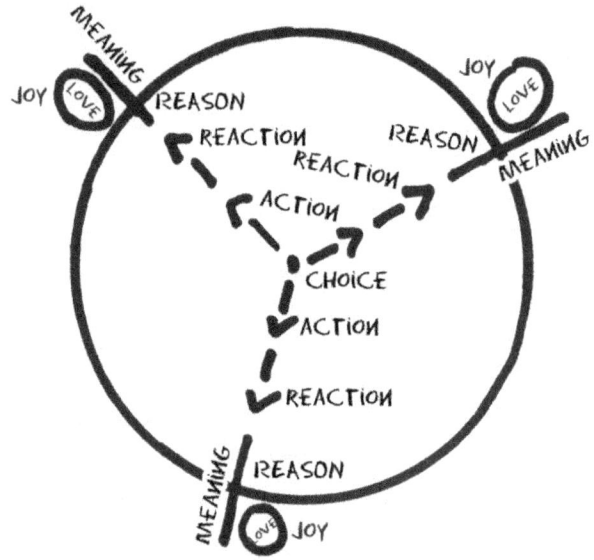

JOY SPHERES ROUNDING THE EARTH

Figure 7Joy spheres. Moments of stillness wrapped around moments of faith in perpetual motion.

Pi are less than squared: pi is not the largest number, even with the longest number path. 3 and the Infinite complimenting each other on balanced point. Forever tangled below 4. Waiting on 1 to be more. The certain mystery of the infinite. The ideal. 3 is still a 3 until you put the whole thing into action as a perspective of measurement in resonated complement to any circle's details to form a more encompassing understanding of any magnitude with just one simple number – all of them.

"HOW MANY FINGERS AM I HOLDING UP?"

"FORE!"

There's a time to talk and a time to write until there's no more time the moment we all understand something. A moment of urgent priority to achieve an understanding of structure around a renewed space full of truth, liberties and justice to live within and among. A moment of faith in perpetual motion – Utopia. Where everything is possible in every number of ways for each everybody everywhere. A forest full of Trees of Good rising up to touch the sun.

SECTION III
Power of the Pyramid

Utopia Exists
In Spite of Monetarists
Where Our Faiths Persist

CHAPTER 2
Faithful Currency

FAITHFUL SOURCES

Genesis of Faith, Wealth and Currency

FAITH   FAITH   FAITH PAID   JOY OF
EARNED   SAVED   FOR HOME   LIFE

When a society forms, the work is exerted for the good of all in a way that is understood unanimously. As immediate safety of time and place are achieved with this work what was once an instinctual certainty becomes a divergence of sincere, singular pursuits seeking their paths to achievement. A proxy means by which we motivate the work exerted and reward the work achieved along paths with unique understandings within a transaction is created – currency backed by faith in the work and credit to the stewards of our wealth. As society matures we grant the inspired a means to appreciate wealth through investments they have come to own by applying their faithful currency to the purchase. This transfer of faith from a concept to a creation is the materialization of good from intention. It takes on a life of its own as a faithful holding through appreciation potential and wealth when interest is achieved. When integrity, progress and willingness to share the path of progress are combined it appreciates the holding with credit for using liberty wisely to invest the original faith.

Hypothetically, uncertainty is the reflection of faithlessness creating the first notions of stress surrounding money. As time moves forward and misunderstood pursuits by our leaders, representatives and employers become common while cyclicality grips their behaviors the public replaces the concept of our currency's faith with the trained expectation of distrust toward what is being done with our money. This uncertainty may lead to disastrous results over time if trained expectations become the new understanding leading to long-term faithlessness. As a result, taxes are collected from the involvements in life we agree are sound – our work.

Taxes are easily understood involvements of faith in currency. They are applied to the misunderstood, debatable or faithless expenditures chosen by our leaders, representatives and organizations as a means to maintain faith flowing from source through to expenditure through to transaction. Taxes are the means of funding debatable projects with the faith of our work for transaction stability.

Having a place to put our savings that provides us with certain consistency when it is not intended to be risked as an investment of potential appreciation is how we take the worry out of money. Lack of worry fosters a certainty inspiring faith, and ultimately trust, when coupled with inspired acts using our money as long as the ongoing risks associated with challenging investments are reasonable ones that will not likely place us in a pit of relentless struggle if risks taken in our name do not lead to reward. Over time, citizen confidence rises in order to foster investment in small business, stocks and real estate with amounts of faith in savings investors wish to become wealth.

> *Consider this: If our money is backed by any finite resource it tends to favor those people alive when it is most available. What about future generations? Gold makes sense if you're selfish. If you think long-term it is a horrible idea. In 1971 the price of an ounce of gold was $35. Forty years later it was over $1700. That's way more profit than the average successful investor makes on the stock market. If you can get a return of over 5000% on your money where is the motivation to invest that money in a business or purchase goods? You would only need to purchase a king-sized mattress to hide all your gold-backed currency! Faithless financial growth for those with extra money to save would benefit at the expense of societal*

expansion. Viewing business investments as more of a risk than simply holding your money is not a good perspective for society to hold.

People are valuable. In a society managed by faith people are the sole asset you can count on to retain their fundamental value over time. Sincere efforts by individuals are the primary means by which faith is created from that value. Individuals need to know how important they are to their society. The genesis of money defines clearly what backs every single dollar the United States of America has printed – the value of every individual citizen earning, spending and investing their faiths while at the same time adding to our collective wealth.

Consider this: *In an ideal example of a society's domestic economic system the amount of wealth in its total wealth pool is equal to the amount of wealth generated by all work and appreciation. The value of that wealth pool is completely stable. Everyone agrees that we are all worth what we are paid in salary. Even those among us with a guilty conscience for our salaries are supported by the faith of an employer or customer who paid that salary for the work performed. The currency generated by work is a faithful amount by unanimous consent of all those entering salary transactions.*

Our appreciated investments are worth what someone will pay for them with their accumulated faith or trade for them with another wealth of their own. That makes wealth increase by appreciation a faithful transaction. Every investment transaction is based upon work done by people so that the investment may faithfully rise in value by agreement of the people involved. The more unanimous the agreement the more certain the value will become more valuable.

Hope guides us out of chaos. Increasing certainty inspires faith. Faith builds into trust over time. In turn, that trust becomes another support for feelings of certainty among the citizens of a society when its secular faith is well-placed within an economy managing faith with integrity and sincerity.

How can we sustain secular faith of every individual as the fundamental faith achieving stable value in currency through time?

I suggest a projection of the better qualities of an individual when achieving wealth through work and investments is the way to maintain maximum faithfulness from the perspective of the individual towards the stewards of our collective wealth pool and the currency that we use to give that wealth its value. Maintaining that underlying value in a stable currency by keeping an eye on management of secular faith within society is a bedrock of all faiths, beliefs and certainties. Immigration of that pool, once understood, becomes a spring eternally renewing our faiths.

> **Consider this:** *Worker A is a painter. He creates forgeries of expensive art and sells them as the genuine painting. When he receives payment for the art he gambles with it at the Poker tables. His work is unfaithful due to the negative personal qualities maintained during the achievement and appreciation of his paintings. If this became public knowledge it would degrade his contribution to the wealth pool with an uncertainty that degrades faith into hope. His own inner sense of faithlessness leads him to give back all that money via the casino where luck gifts his conscience with a more faithful transaction.*
>
> *Worker B is a gold prospector. He wakes early to begin work at the stream. He works until sunset then washes and vials his nuggets for trading at the gold exchange. He receives cash at the current market value for his gold. His excess earnings are used to purchase savings bonds. The value of his wealth is faithful due to the positive personal qualities and integrities maintained during the achievement of his work and appreciation of the gold from its valueless source in the stream to valuable in his hands once his work expenditure recovers the gold from the Earth. His wealth inspires a high degree of faith. His inner sense of faith in his own work leads him to place the rewards of his work in an investment of long-term perspective with a high degree of certainty.*

Imagine a nation full of workers achieving like Worker A. Unfaithful sources of currency and unfaithful expenditures carry high risk degrading the stability of your wealth. In many nations around the world the lack of faith in currency has eroded creating volatility or collapse at one time or another. Stewards of that nation's wealth acting with unfaithful behavior have contributed to complete collapse of currency value by faithlessness leading to resonating, or self-deprecating, collapse of every individual's personal faith in their own future as savings, investments and the relative value of their work erode right before their eyes.

Now imagine a nation full of workers that achieve like Worker B. When positive qualities are predominant in wealth creation they support the value of your wealth with faith, belief and certainty over time.

When a nation provides environments inspiring behavior improvement to occur with the consent of each citizen inspired to do so it is a show of faith toward each individual that leadership believes in each citizen's value to society. As the population improves and exemplifies a depth and breadth of positive qualities – including the leadership and representation structures of government – feelings of faith, stability and certainty among the population will increase and reflect themselves in the certain stability of our collective wealth.

Taxing Faith

As leaders and representatives free themselves from the burdens of ongoing elimination of harm by handing their solutions over to authorities and enforcement agencies they look toward what else they may do within our environment of progress. These projects are often viewed as positive action by some and negative action by others. Situations such as preemptive war – looking for moments to act outside our boundaries to achieve further harm reduction within - may even find themselves with a constituency in the minority compared to those who believe in them. Over time, whether external involvements are effective at their goals or not the fact remains that the general public no longer sees clearly the effect of harm reduction in front of them when there is not much harm to reduce. Continued spending of secular faith in such a way might collapse a nation's currency value over time as every transaction contributing to war is considered a build-up of faithlessness.

In the United States, our deeply debatable involvements such as conflict resolution overseas have not contributed to a decline in faith of our currency. This is due to the fact that taxes have been used to pay for them. Taxes are the surest form of Faithful Currency Source – the integrity of everyone's work. We do not question the value of the underlying currency used for debatable transactions when there is a correlation to the faithfulness of everyone's work as the source of payment.

FAITHFUL EXPENDITURES

What about situations in which the expenditure is full of faith? Does the transaction remain faithful if the money comes directly from a verifiable government printing press? I suggest it does as long as the expenditure is one which we all agree to through our representatives by Unanimous Consent. Unanimous Consent is the surest form of Faithful Expenditure – the integrity of what works for everyone. Just like our work, we all agree that the currency involved is backed by active faith in the expenditure.

THE PROGRESS EVERYONE CAN AGREE ON BECOMES THE CERTAINTY EVERYONE WILL BELIEVE IN.

FAITHFUL TRANSACTIONS

The key to giving Utopian Capitalism perpetual motion carrying it beyond its inspired moment of faith is a stable currency value. The certainty that an individual's wealth gained from work and investment will be safe when held in the currency of a nation creates a trust that future work and investment in that nation will be worth the effort for an individual to attempt.

All workers will agree they earn their salary. Their employers agree that they are worth it too. Salaries are a very faithful expenditure when they are paid out. Therefore, if we allow our government to simply print the money it needs every year to pay salaries to workers providing us with our commonwealths that transaction is a faithful one.

FAITHFUL SOURCE OR FAITHFUL EXPENDITURE = FAITHFUL TRANSACTION

Sources of money inspire faith when they are based on work and appreciation. Expenditures of money inspire faith when they are paid with faithful sources of money or when they complete transactions of faithful work and appreciation managed by government and organizations we have extended unanimous consent to do so.

CHAPTER 3
Strengthening Structure with Inspiration Opportunities

REACTIVE STRUCTURE

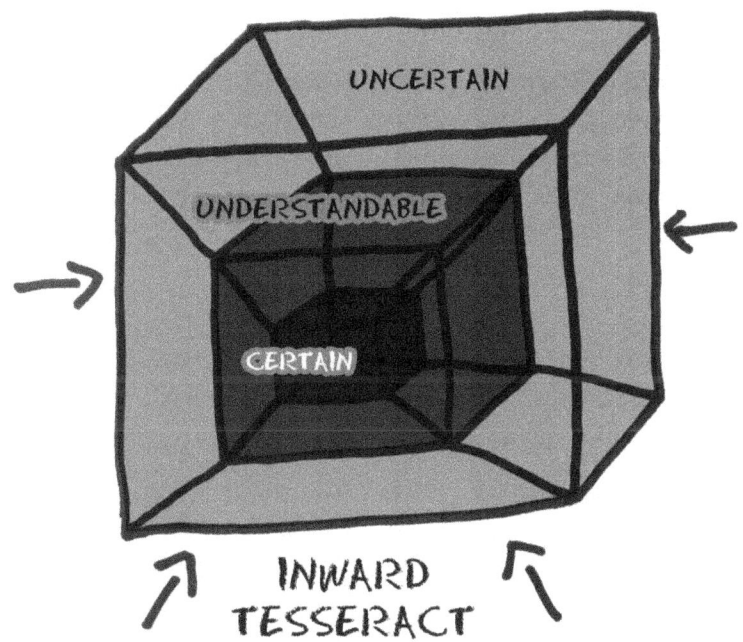

When progress in our personal lives is put on hold for the sake of what must be done to maintain control of our life's direction we are stuck in a whirlpool or an inward tesseract. This metaphor indicates a burden or struggle which is too heavy for our outward progress to bear. As the world's policeman, the United

States is often putting progress on hold for the sake of what must be done, not only for itself, but also for the rest of the world. This ostensible show of strength through militarization is perhaps the greatest weakness to a path of planned progress – or any progress.

In a reactive environment, there are few means of exerting our consciousness. Reaction to circumstances such as violence, poverty, threats and intimidation, humiliation, hopelessness and other negative involvements with life is never better than the first time it is experienced. Over a length of time, the stress we endure in making choices according to a plan with emotional intelligence can lead to a trained reactiveness of logical strategy that forgets how to plan at all when reinforced by the emotional harm below the minimum standard of struggle we are willing to live within to avoid the risk of reentering it. In other words, we tread water just below the surface with the hope that we might periodically bob up for air while minimizing the chance that we will succumb to the strength of the whirlpool's cycle without considering how easy it may be to simply float on our backs until a way of exiting the whirlpool becomes clear.

As a reflection of our collective personal struggles the United States federal and state governments also suffer from the effect of the strong metaphors that resonate inward and down from our military actions around the world. Change of a dwindling cyclical nature keeps issues of national and regional prominence reoccurring within our societal landscape. Ultimately, the strength of the whirlpool has trapped us all.

MEANINGFUL STRUCTURE

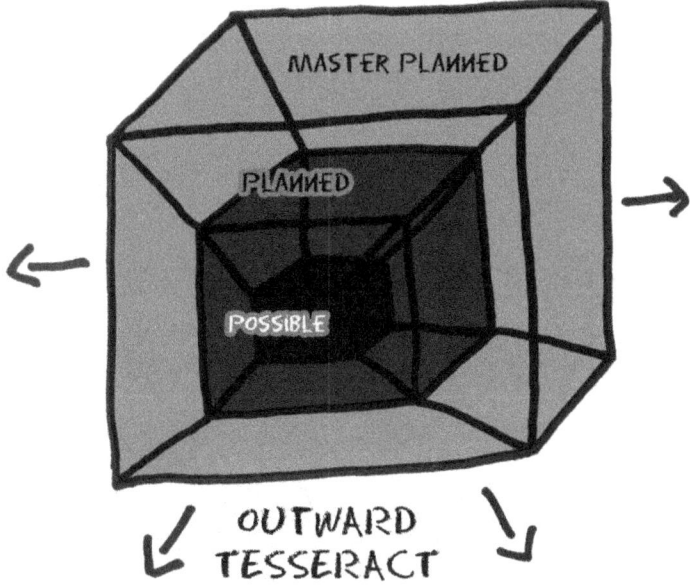

When personal paths to success are marked by others in ways we can follow to achieve our own successful outcomes we are safe inside a meaningful structure of logical steps. Metaphorically, we are inside of a well-defined box sitting at its center. This feels like freedom. Over time, however, as all of the paths become well-worn they get broken down into steps catering to superior outcomes that anyone with the will might achieve. Rules and regulation hold such a box of being together in progressive cyclicality. They are rigid standards of behavior that may or may not continue their relevance over time. The odd pairing of standards which become more relevant in our perception from the inside riding along with standards which become more irrelevant from the outside looking in can skew the box into other shapes. A pyramid perhaps.

A pyramid is an organized structure of superior thought creating certainty for those at the bottom or middle making their ways up. Yet if those already at the top of their facets feel as though there is nowhere else to go for themselves it is an indication of problems. As indications grow more plentiful over time they become warnings. The certainty of a clear view from the top becomes cloudy as more and more dreams are diminished. A society structured around a box of being that finds itself attempting to operate from a whirlpool mentality is in particular danger of a relative few at the top losing their understanding of the many at the bottom. Those who find themselves outside the pyramid all together in the whirlpool of struggles with no faith that they will ever again re-enter the safety of the pyramid may give up trying and opt to build their own structure. In practical terms, this results in the permanent fracturing of society.

COMPASSIONATE STRUCTURE

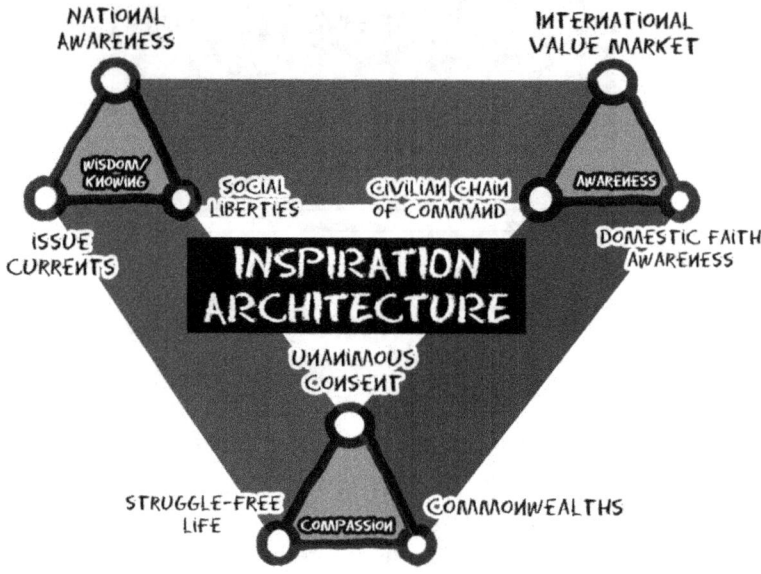

Figure 8Inspiration Architecture. This framework supportive of a belief structure renews reactive mentalities into proactive and pre-emptive compassion.

I suggest re-opening the outer boundaries of our skewed box with a spring – a Jack-In-The-Box! This time around that means more than simply a new technological innovation or any other level of detail perspective shifts. This time we will open the box with a structural perspective that reflects not only who many of us already feel we are as citizens of the world but also a framework and a glimpse at who we are in the future as we renew our pledge to lead the world in structure among the compassionate societies on Earth. To do so responsibly requires a renewed sense of purpose from our smallest structural metaphor – the eye at the top. That means a renewal of the principles upon which we guide our societal choices. I suggest the addition of compassion to the Golden Rule is all it takes to turn it into the Aquarian Principle. In other words, the notion that choices we assert upon our environments are necessarily chosen by awareness of perspectives outside of our own.

APPROVE WHEN YOU CAN, ACCEPT WHEN YOU CAN'T, DO NO HARM AS YOU DO.

Translating metaphor to practical terms this indicates a hands-off approach to guidance from our society as we embark on the expanding cyclicality of a wellspring rising from outside and below the pyramid to emerge rising and around from within with aeration jets dancing atop it. When balanced by intention, wisdom and open, sincere communication it might also be metaphorically akin to the clouds opening up to reveal a Heaven on earth. Utopia.

YOU CAN'T LEAD A FAITHFUL POPULATION IF YOU DEMAND TO BELIEVE EVERYTHING FIRST. MANAGEMENT OF LEADERSHIP IMPEDES THE FLOW OF FAITH RETURNING TO THE PEOPLE WHO BELIEVE IN YOU.

To avoid such a happening is literally a build-up of pressure from the struggles being held within the box of being. Achieving movement again as the tesseract flows outward is akin to the opening of a valve in a sprinkler releasing water for the grass learning to grow green and tall and out as what lies in the water's path becomes shade for the future grass in the sand nearby to grow as well. This all becoming a new pyramid with a Chia-seeded lawn on and around it and joys of life rolling like blossoming tumbleweeds in the sun! In practical metaphor, the stability that results over time as we allow the Eye of Providence to "blink" is synonymous with pyramids the Chinese government has covered up with earth to let the green grass grow with a sprinkler on top. The ebb and flow of life in our world.

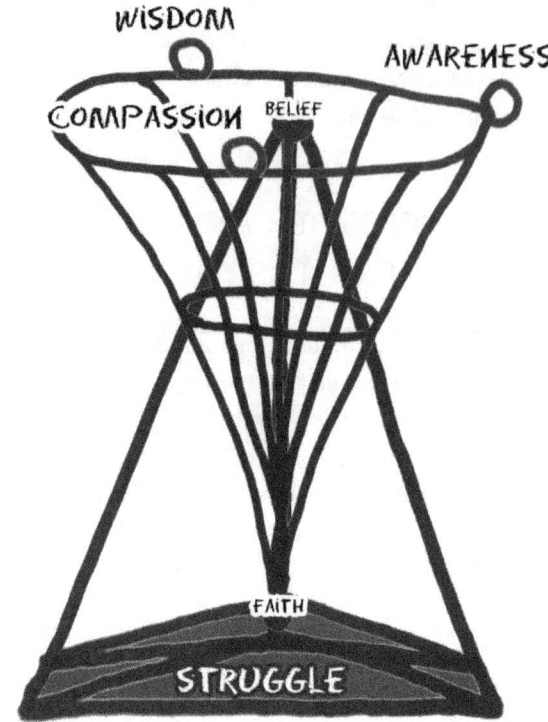

FAITH SUPPORTING BELIEF (STRUCTURE IN THE MAKING)

INSPIRED ENVIRONMENTS OF PROGRESS

TRUTH IS THE POWER. EXPRESSING IT MEANINGFULLY IS A MARK OF THE POWERFUL.

To achieve such aims I suggest our society must improve its trust of, and willingness to collaborate with, artists possessing an ideal excellence or sincere inspired motivation in their chosen art. An environment encompassing inspired environments of apprenticeship; each one of them based upon the structures artists choose for so long as we all agree with the guidance of compassionate principles and act upon them.

CHAPTER 4
Emotional Intelligence

NATIONAL AWARENESS

Domestic Agencies

As our modern history of strategies to move us up and down give way to plans that move us out and around it becomes important to reconsider agencies and interests within our society that serve as intelligence in service to strategy. Strategy is indicative of competition. For frontrunners that means over time you run out of places to lay your strategy once your chosen competitions are complete. In the past, agencies of security have protected us from violence and intimidation.

Once we are no longer intimidated for lack of those aggressors in our world I suggest a reinvention of national security as national awareness to meet the needs of a more responsible nation interested in master planning its future is a necessity. If we can agree that national security is focused upon identification of threats we might also agree that national awareness is the ability to predict and understand the internal and external environment of threatening people and groups in the context of present circumstances to prevent them from becoming threats at all.

When security shifts from primarily means of acting upon people to means of actions to shape the environments in which people involve themselves it is a clear sign that national awareness is taking place. Creation of inspiration environments with intent to keep responsible plans within the boundaries of our master planning become a valuable resource of national awareness agencies as they gather ambiguous intelligence of environmental factors along with intelligence timelines in order to turn deduction into prediction with no erosion of personal rights while doing so.

At the level of international involvement awareness agencies find themselves defining our perspective on national personalities around the world, the opportunity environments offering America complementary paths of progress within them and an improving sense of our own contributions among an inspired collection of world interests expressing themselves through economic, social and master planning involvements. Correlating components of our own Wealth Pool to organizations defining our expanding boundaries of social liberty provides a framework of emotional intelligence ideals from which we derive details of our own national personality guiding domestic understanding and international awareness by calculable means.

International Mediation

The Middle East peace processes have not traditionally been a success. For forty years they have failed. I have a suggestion that can be relevant for any future peace accord anywhere in the world. Do not merely make peace - create something.

The major error in former peace accords has been the absence of something to do with the peace that is made. Perhaps after decades of war nations and societies at war do not even know!

> **Consider this**: *If you have been at war for forty years and your population is made up of all 39 years old or younger citizens, nobody will remember how to maintain peaceful living. Planning for what will be created on top of the foundation of peace is essential to take focus off the peace itself so that perspectives on creation may take shape from all responsible angles. After all, watching the peace can only create debate on details jeopardizing the peace.*

What happens if the peace slips back into struggle? Outlining a plan for either or both sides to re-initiate peace without the need for a new discussion is essential in our modern era of media distortion and dirty tricks by interested third parties. Creating a plan of steps that cannot be mistaken for anything but sincerity is one way around manipulations that seek to keep war a present-day nuisance.

> *Don't forget, "Mr. Gorbachev, tear down this wall!" Take a picture. It will last longer. Bring video, cameras and invite people from around the globe who will take word of the peace back with them.*

Tactical Peacekeeping

As the Earth becomes a more consistently peaceful place to live we ought give some thought to what our military can transition to in competence to bridge the gap between harm limitation and exploratory inspiration. Management of the peace left in our stead or our wake is one potential.

THERE IS NO ALLEGIANCE IN PATRIOTISM MORE IMPORTANT THAN TO PEACE.

Tactical Peacekeeping is my phrase for a system of psychological awareness in creation of unique context manipulations of aggressive environments risking return to chaos, or smaller regional conflicts, that can be surrounded by the tactics. By setting up a graph of a society's environment trends, individual perspective flexibility and structural perspectives on action it remains only to start at the top and bottom of these facets and pinch the society – briefly – in the middle with a reasonable struggle requiring only civilian authority to manage calm. Then ease the push from the bottom back to the "zero" edge and exit the circumstance while leaving behind support and gifted outcomes that match the steps and achievements of meaningful repair to the population.

In the example below, the perspectives of a society which are relevant to a context of progress and most susceptible to the harm of war are shown.

SOCIETY'S ENVIRONMENT	INDIVIDUAL PERSPECTIVES			GOVERNMENTAL CONCERNS
	TIME	PLACE	PRIORITY	
ANARCHY				
CHAOS				
SAVAGERY OF WAR	THE MOMENT	WHERE YOU STAND	LIVING	PREVENTION OF DISSOLUTION
STRUGGLES TO 'ZERO'	SHORT-TERM GOALS	WHERE YOUR HOME IS	CONSISTENT WELL-BEING	PRINCIPLES / ORGANIZATION / ORDER / PROCESSES
COMMON EXERTIONS	CYCLICAL GOALS	CITY / STATE	SATISFACTION / FUN	SERVICES / RIGHTS / LIBERTIES
CHALLENGES	LONG-TERM GOALS	NATION/ WORLD	FUN / JOYS OF LIFE	SUPPORT OF MASTERPLANNING
BALANCE				
WELFARE	CYCLICAL CONSUMPTION	CITY / STATE	SATISFACTION / FUN	SCRUTINY AND CYCLICAL CHANGE OF MANAGED FACETS

If a Tactical Peacekeeping force takes a position to stabilize (or penalize) this society they now have a more effective alternative to fighting or enforcement – shared, meaningful struggle with a path and the means to rise above it.

1. Consider the personality facets of a nation, region or conflict zone. Determine the milestones of progress from chaos or war to civilian modes of struggle. What are the symbols indicative of those milestones? What are the associated practical improvements and tangible achievements in civilian society? What added responsibilities and honors are adopted by people on such a path to better living? Keep these complementary lists handy.

2. Devise a military theatric of sights, sounds and tumbles of chaos to surround the troubled area, if possible. Keep such a distance that no one is hurt yet close enough to administer an emotional toll to potential fighters through remembrance of war and peer pressure of the civilians among them anticipating the same. Cycle the theatric to give the audience time to consider it. Along the lines of your milestones list, decrease the emotional toll towards a more civilian feel of struggle in deliberate steps recognizable to those who consider them in the society.

3. Augment this theatric with propaganda and non-lethal force at a distance to change the tone of war to mere struggle. Propaganda that includes an historical timeline of the diminishment of their struggle

serves dual use as a step-by-step chart to understand for those who may otherwise suffer PTSD if they are merely placed within an outcome of peaceful civility rather than walk it themselves in their minds holding hands with their emotional healing and the certainty of role models – real or made for illustration of the points – placed along the steps to peace. Creation of the heroes of the peace in advance of the warring factions creating heroes of the fight makes a better narrative for history.

4. Simultaneous with this movement away from chaos is the need to raise the floor temporarily. Consider the humble beginnings of the United States colonies. Pioneers were aware of each other's perspective on struggle as they sought to keep the wild environment behind a fence they had rushed to build. Or the cold air out with the fireplace of their cabins. Needs were understood and instinctive. By removing the opportunity for challenges and distracting conflicts while raising the floor up to mid-struggle level the society being surrounded becomes "pinched" into a potential to share perspectives similar to the colonial pioneers in America. All victims of war are likely suffering from single-mindedness and reactivity. Determining a "struggle project" for them to work on and providing the means to achieving success – including the tangible items such as building materials, heavy equipment, printing presses – is the final act in this step.

5. Back your military involvement out, if reasonable, once the means and the steps are understood.

Consider this: A village decimated by war has lost its infrastructure completely. It's the last holdout of rebel fighters. What rebels need to feel whole is a cause. What more noble cause than to be involved with the rebuilding of a society akin to the re-founding of a nation. It's an opportunity to lay down their weapons and write their place in national history when they lead the use of the means your military has left behind to quickly re-build government and justice facilities to support policing, school buildings, water distribution locations, communications and transportation. These are meaningful reasons to expel many more military personnel with advanced degrees in civil engineering and psychology as they architect

> *unique struggle projects to fit areas of violent hopelessness in need.*

In this example, once the struggle to repair infrastructure is concluded and the lower barrier to challenges is removed the society will have the steps in mind and the renewed faith built on achievement it needs to continue toward prosperity alone. The shared perspective achieved in the struggle project creates a moment of awareness crossing divides of ethnic or ideological misunderstanding. A meaningful attempt fully competent to lay the groundwork for future miracles to occur when dreamt.

It's important to note that forcible placement of a war-torn populace into a successful mindset without understandings of the steps to get there from a chaotic circumstance can backfire into post-traumatic stress if the change is held and resentment or further hopelessness if it is taken away. In either case the success is not achieved if it is not achieved in the minds of the people involved. The pride of rebuilding a homeland or one's birthplace is a strong motivation for rebellions to move on from fighting in agreement.

A break in the tempo of relentless intimidation with a symphony of sounds from the human condition was a wonderful attempt by the Russian Military Orchestra and the Red Army Choir in Syria. They achieved an inspiration more potent than a bomb. The wailing sounds of misery find their role model in the violin as they learn once again to ascend from their depths on the staircase of those notes. Perhaps another, smoother stairway out of Hell we will add to our arsenals of peacekeeping around the world.

ISSUE CURRENTS

Issue Currents are a new form of PAC which defines a broad interest of society led by formerly elected and appointed officials in order to lobby, innovate and improve upon them across a long segment of time. In this way, they are political parties for issues as they stitch ongoing ideals into long-term success of the nation. I suggest a great way to form them is by correlation to the committees of the House of Representatives and Senate and the master planning milestone achievements of the Executive Branch.

In a Utopian cycle of change toward meaningful conclusions and back again there are necessarily groups of citizen ideals without priority or urgency which become more important over time. Ideals with priority in the past serve as strong wisdoms of perspective gained from their conclusive results. Perseverance of former leaders and stewards maintains interest of those citizens involved in championing those ideals and a sense of ongoing responsible behavior as they are led to new ideals following successful outcomes – to build a staircase upon them. This prevents fractures from forming by role modeling collaboration of multiple perspectives around single ideals of issue. Issue Currents maintain a connection among complementary paths of improvement and renewal reflecting the complementary linear means of multistage achievements.

Issue currents allow our finest leaders and representatives to maintain support of their ideals – preventing the corporate sector from replacing their perspectives of personal value in political office with a desk of corporate whim in order to catch up their wealth to those who have not served the public interest. Interest groups then find their niche and value to an Issue Current in order to achieve support in Washington D.C. In this way, the wise hold on to and improve their wisdom according to their ideals and create a more meaningful position for themselves at the tops of mountains awaiting the next gondola lift of corporate seekers to match with new perspectives in Congress and achievements of Executive Master Planning guided by their expertise and perspectives.

Issue currents are better gatekeepers than traditional lobbyists. Officials of former public prominence prevent issues of too fine a detail from entering political discussion in the wrong venue. They are also better means of distributing election contributions for people interested in voting by ideal rather than according to urgencies of choice or personality contests. Once gathered, the elder statesmen of our nation will routinely distribute campaign donations from the issue current to politicians of any party or independence. Issues that have fulfilled their promises naturally wane along with citizen donations and interest. While issues of necessity gather the strength they need over time to rally former statesmen around them with the wisdom to carry them through to meaningful fruition within the current Congress.

SOCIAL LIBERTIES

Social Liberties Department

IDEAL LEADERSHIP IS THE ONE VOICE THAT ANSWERS ALL VOICES IN QUESTION AND SPEAKS FOR ALL VOICES IN REPLY.

Lack of an ideal social architecture to renew the dogmatic certainties of the past has left us with social justices reacting to social injustices as the norm all know without offering any new actions to raise the mean line of social liberties. It is fitting that we give Social Liberties a lifetime appointment to a cabinet-level position. The time when harmed groups can be identified by ethnicity or gender alone is over.

Social Liberties is a preemptive civil rights department based upon expectation that we may alleviate harm in advance through awareness of how our master planned society will adjust to improvements, progress and natural flow of collective personality awareness. Harm prevention is defined by its opposite – awareness support – and defended by our previous wisdoms reflected upon and reflected into determinations of legislation and rulings founded on principle.

If we are convinced that we are different then we are, but if we feel the same we complement who each of us can be with parallel lives seeking joy. As reflections and metaphors of inspired awareness take the place of security and limitation organizations within our government the Civil Liberties Department will be the role model we look to for an understanding of the difference.

THE DIFFERENCE THAT IT MAKES IS THE DEFERENCE THAT IT TAKES.

With respect and appreciation for the diverse landscape of social involvements that have built themselves upon the maturing structure of civil rights and the wisdoms that protect people from harm using racial, ethnic, religious, gender or age-based criteria we will re-invent the concept of rights and liberties for the next century.

Our current methods of preemptive harm reduction are based on reactivity to crime, discrimination or other unforeseen superiority behavior. They require someone be harmed prior to defining the means of their security which allows civil rights abuse to lead its own prevention. Social Liberties define concepts of liberty based on our foresight into matters of human involvement which may result in superiority harm to groups of citizens defining themselves along lines of their collective choice in parallels that fit within our established principles and understood respects for human life. Identifying these social groups as they emerge is a key step in creation of inspiration environments promoting behavior improvement with individual awareness.

Supreme Court Vulturing

Hand in hand with the ability to foresee harm is the capability to rule against that harm in advance. Allowing the Supreme Court to vulture its own cases from the many avenues of information it receives through a civilian chain of command is an essential part of the Social Liberties concept. Taking action to enshrine rights and privileges in advance of any harm done to a single citizen is the mark of a maturing society worthy of the label Utopian.

CHAPTER 5
Sincere Communication

INTERNATIONAL VALUE MARKET

In war, a tie goes to the winners that avoid it. Some experts suggest that World War III will be a financial war between nations. If that's true, then it will be a war of faith against faith. In that sense, it makes no sense! War is a faithless pursuit. I suggest there is an easy way to avoid World War III or any financially-weaponized conflict - perspective.

It's important to remember that currency value, when not backed by an investment material, is an agreement among citizens of a nation. Internationally, the relative value is currently out of national control even though international value is a completely national decision. Not a true value at all without a basis to be found domestically. More akin to the stock market roller coaster than a measure of a nation's faith in government stewardship of its wealth and wealth potential.

Communicating the understood domestic perspectives and international perspectives on currency as a standard of differentiation to every citizen is all that it takes to guard against using FOREX markets and other international financial instruments as a means of undermining faith held in domestic currencies. Setting the expectation that international values will rise and fall, but domestic consistency is expected to maintain stability for the long-term is what citizens expect their leaders to explain to them when they are informed enough to understand that their national currency is a component of social structure as well as financial and economic structures.

International valuation of nations in service to relative currency value creates a meaningful and transparent method of value with a bonus: a financial vehicle of limited risk and steady growth. Consider an international exchange of national value underlying currency run by the WTO, World Bank or similar organization of world credibility conceptually like international savings bonds with known rates, risks and expiration time periods. The profit made in the exchange will finance the oversight operations of national value used to set baseline currency value around the world while allowing anyone to easily invest in a foreign country's long-term success.

This is the means for a developing country to support a faithful foreign currency supply to complement their tax base in reinvesting their potential while building trust in their domestic currency stability. It's a safer means, from the domestic perspective, for nations and individuals to invest in a nation and for that nation to be invested in without being purchased. A super-charged savings bond of a more liquid nature will thrive in a world of nations supportive of each other's' progress.

I suggest the United Nations will be the clearing house of all the career and production multipliers that affect national valuations of member states for international trade purposes. Each country may still enter treaties, economic unions and free trade agreements. Yet as the multipliers of world master planning become more useful and meaningful to a world of Capitalist Utopias springing up to end poverty and stabilize domestic faith a third-party oversight by a trusted organization will give national valuations even more credibility than the faith already achieved from the work and appreciable investments they are based on.

The World Trade Organization will be the custodian of plans drawn up by the U.N. as well as arbiter and watchdog for countries that wish to work their treaties and agreements through that organization.

The World Bank will still provide loans; however, those loans will be in instances of faithless populations that have recently overcome war, coup d'état, natural disaster or other calamities that destabilize faith fundamentally. Third world nations moving to Infinite Currency for the first time might also benefit from a collaboration of currency from a neighboring country without the potential for destabilization present in some countries at inception. In such cases, the World Bank will manage cross-border transfer between economic unions to ensure integrity.

Mediator banks are also needed in cases of:

- International workers paid in their own currency
- Aid from other nations
- Aid to other nations

From year to year the domestic total wealth pool will be reported to the World Bank and WTO first. Each organization will run domestic figures through their own calculations to total gains in relation to career and production multiplied figures. Irregularities trigger warnings to the United Nations when domestic fraud may be occurring.

Each year the "safe zone" of wealth value increase will change not only on variables of domestic standing but also on the current range and ratios in countries of similar circumstance at that time. Situations such as natural disaster, major infrastructure projects and world master planning contributions will be accounted for within these minimums and maximums. This system gives nations a pair of third-party oversights that will alert them to corruption unnoticed domestically.

The United Nations will then be informed after the WTO and World Bank verify their calculations with each other and the nation in question. In no event will penalties be assessed for domestic supplies increasing with consent of the government. Yet just as sanctions are put in place today for potential to violence, potential to currency fraud will sandbox willful state offenders. Power-focused politicians will disappear quickly as the gift of Infinite Currency attracts better behavior not only from the citizenry but also from existing leadership and representation.

One Standard – All Of Them

I suggest one standard of underlying value be adopted – every standard. International value reporting will be done from the perspective of every national currency so that long-term statistics will be easily understood by citizens of every nation without converting their currency unit value to dollars or pounds first. A fundamental determination of domestic buying power for a single unit of currency is all it takes.

Remember, this faith and credit is all a part of a domestic perspective on currency. International perspectives on the relative value of a nation's currency are separate and should never have the ability to undermine what a nation's currency value stability has achieved for itself. Creation of a world-wide method and complementary systems for determining relative values of national currency units overseen by organizations in which all countries have faith is the key to maintaining integrity among international currency values. Expressing those values in terms of each country's own currency looking outward is essential.

Credibility and Priority Ratings

Credibility ratings are reflections of faithful sources and faithful expenditures within the International Value Markets. Priority ratings are reflections of liberties with time – tariffs for compound trading. Utilizing these and other reflections of stock market integrity within a system predicated on the faithful progress of nations emerging to a Utopian understanding make International Value Market-based investments an attractive option for institutional and other wealth-managed entities.

DOMESTIC FAITH AWARENESS

An active and passive system of domestic intelligence focused upon understanding levels of happiness around the country will be created and maintained. In order to avoid "1984"-style big brother tactics the information gathered will be voluntary and indirect so that no one can be directly identified by the information unless they choose to be. Information will be reported in the granularity of a city block or a country square mile in a real-time database accessible by every Congressman and Senator.

Spending Habits

Reporting from supermarkets and convenience stores detailing the daily purchasing habits of people they serve will give a glimpse into how they feel without revealing identity. Increases in alcoholic beverage purchases, for example, may be an indication experts can correlate to a building stress in the area.

Census Questionnaires

As the public becomes comfortable sharing their feelings with a government that acts only to inspire them for it the ability to simply ask plain-spoken questions to the general public as an optional section of the U.S. Census will become a standard of data collection for ongoing happiness in America. Development of the means to verifiably submit data to the government electronically will allow census information to be taken more frequently. The study of this data and all of the ways in which we may support ongoing inspiration in America from known points of emotional wellness will emerge as a particularly important psychological skill.

Faith Dashboard

Every Congressman and Senator will have access to a real-time electronic report, or dashboard, of their districts and states in order to identify areas requiring their action. This is a gift for all representatives seeking cues to guide their scheduled communication with constituents. At the end of every focus upon an area's faith loss will be the personal narratives and Congressional involvements seeking to mitigate negative outcomes with positive inspirations or meaningful management of the environment.

CIVILIAN CHAIN OF COMMAND

A closed social network for elected officials and other government leaders that creates a web of nodes denoting in-person acquaintance, hierarchy and clearance allowing information to be sent to each member of the network from any other with a pre-existing credibility. This civilian chain of any command allows information to be passed through human filtering to eliminate unnecessary communication, improve the context of information with notes and attachments, allow timely delivery of messages outside of agenda and create an accountability path that is human verifiable. In times of crisis this network functions as a communication lifeline capable of isolating breaches with simple human accountability while maintaining an efficiency supported through encryption technologies.

In support of Social Liberties and Supreme Court Vulturing this system creates a dedicated channel of filtered information that updates urgency, priority and content according to the judgment of the human beings in the chain who look over the narratives along the way. In this way, issues of consequence to emerging social groups or individuals that indicate a growing harm in our society can be dealt with pre-emptively by predicting how the harm may grow and eliminating the possibility through guidance, legislation or pre-emptive ruling as seen fit.

ONLY HINDSIGHT BENEFITS FROM FOLLOWERS INTERPRETING THEIR LEADERSHIP. FORESIGHT RELIES ON PLAINSPOKEN UNDERSTANDINGS.

This system allows dissemination of communication from members of the network to points of media or other citizen contact with the same measure of oversight and collaborative filtering in order to manage relevant facets of perspective on communication prior to outside interpretation. By specifying nodes along the path to outlets, official communications achieve multi-faceted meaning according to the perspectives involved in shaping the understanding along the way.

CHAPTER 6
Ideal Understanding

COMMONWEALTHS

Commonwealths are the circumstances, services and benefits we expect wherever we go in our nation. The concept of how we all agree is enshrined in our commonwealths such as police departments, fire crews, electric services, water, libraries, news and weather services. While there may be arguments in many perspectives around how we outfit a police force or what books we will purchase for a library there is no denying we all agree on the people and the salaries needed to achieve these circumstances for ourselves wherever we live or travel in America. Therefore, commonwealths are subsidizable in perpetuity.

Our very first Unanimous Consent is every commonwealth salary in the United States paid in full with brand new currency from the most faithful source in America – all of us who say so. No taxes required. In order to achieve additional commonwealths in the future we need a state and federal system of concentric collaborative consent which can unanimously agree to permanent collective desires in our national interest.

UNANIMOUS CONSENT

Faithful Expenditures

Unanimous Consent is civil reverence for the political ritual that creates it and for the people that it serves when sincerity, integrity and timeliness of its patriotism support commonwealths inspiring faith to new heights. Statesmen reemerge in Congress as the metaphor of a successful issue involvement transitions from one of winning by majority to ties going to the winners when we all agree. Unanimous Consent of our Congressmen, Senators, the President and Vice-President give the green light for creation of brand new currency to fund our most Faithful Expenditures from the most Faithful Source – all of us saying so by our leaders and representatives.

Faithful Expenditures by Unanimous Consent inspire our Representatives to work more closely with their districts, each other and the White House in mind more as project managers writing a proposal than mathematicians attempting to make numbers fit before the public interest takes shape. Pork barreling, writing bills in segments that lose funding or projects that grow too large for the original budget to maintain are a thing of the past when projects gain the consent required for all the money their successful conclusions require to come about. When we have the people, the plan and the patience to work together unanimously we will always have the currency to see our projects through to success without the burden of taxes affecting the timeliness of our choices. When reactivity to budget constraints becomes a thing of the past active participation in bills becomes focused upon structural components leaving more details available for delegation to state and local officials.

Concentric Collaborative Consent

Artistry of a single statesman influences the entire representative system for a moment as state congresses and the U.S. Congress all share a stillness of being overpowering the entire system with empowerment. Concentric Collaborative Consent allows a state congress to unanimously nominate a new commonwealth to be shared with the entire nation. Once the U.S. Congress votes on the initiation of the newest tax-free right from society to itself it is sent to all other state congresses for their unanimous consent. In this way, the spring renews itself from the bottom, the top and all around.

STRUGGLE-FREE LIFE

Utopian Capitalism perfects the notion of what a society can do for itself without telling them what to do. It does so by providing the opportunity and freedom to accomplish any of life's challenges. When a person recognizes their own ability to avoid struggle and is certain that that ability will be available in the future without end it frees them to consider which of society's opportunities they will challenge themselves to achieve next. Utopian

Capitalism is based upon the certain ability of every citizen to avoid struggle in the Capitalist way – possessing the money required.

Struggle-free Life is a way that society may offer itself the time, calm and awareness it needs for individuals to achieve their joy of life while improving themselves and their communities. Struggle-free Life is a modular societal perspective that leads to many benefits for every citizen as well as government and authorities of justice.

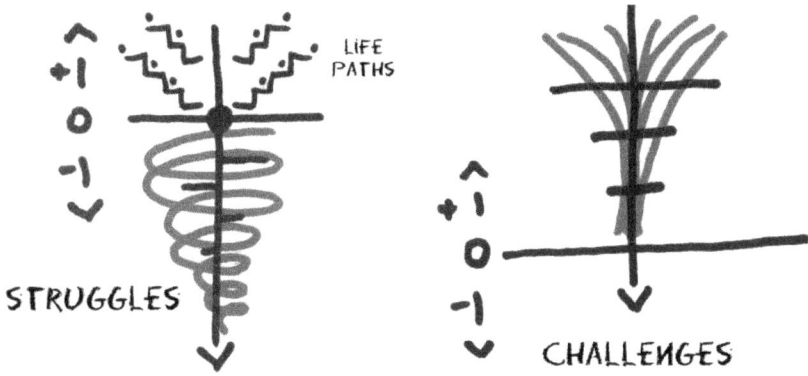

Understanding Struggle-free Life is easy. First, recognize the difference between struggles and challenges. Struggles are problems, distractions and harms that arise unforeseen. Overcoming them achieves nothing on your life path. Think of the movie "Caddy Shack". Remember the gopher? When the gopher emerges to steal the golf ball from the golfer preparing to hit it on his way to his goal that is a metaphor for struggle. Cyclical struggle will destroy motivation to take on challenges leading to meaningful life achievements. In other words, when you look back on years of trying to reach a goal and you have not much to show for your effort it can lead you to avoid trying again.

FORESIGHT LEADING
WITH COMPASSION

HINDSIGHT MAKING LATERAL MOVES

Challenges are the momentary hurdles we overcome on the way to achievements that build motivation to continue achieving. We often prepare for challenges. We typically choose the time, place and duration of our challenges. Challenges met and successfully overcome are seen as a great achievement by those around us when we reach our milestones.

Struggles are the unforeseen setbacks that require us to consider our previous states of being as steps of accomplishment back to zero. The ways back are well documented and share a common sense of renewal while leading to nothing new. The steps we take with forethought have lesser meaning as they fill in gaps left by others on the same journey with similar arcs to similar plateaus as those before. Yet the abundance of build-up of these repetitive arcs in the sea of a society stricken with growing struggles over time becomes its own shared understanding upon which we may base a shared path toward true progress responsibly and with increasing certainty of achievement.

Every path to our goals and joy of life in America contains not only the challenges we anticipate but a few struggles we did not see coming. Struggle-free Life is not the end of challenges. Instead, it is the balance of our society's concern for those overwhelmed by cyclical struggle with respect for each individual's choices along their challenging personal path to their goals. Struggle-free Life is the renewal of the premise that our society truly supports life, liberty and the pursuit of happiness.

Now that you understand the difference between struggles and challenges, consider the choices available to you in a country that ensures your liberties and freedoms such as the United States of America. This environment of respect for ourselves and each other sets the stage for moving along the upward arc of progress in a meaningful way.

> **Consider this:** Think of the end of that arc as a flag indicating the placement of the cup on a golf green. Each one of us is free to hit our ball in any way, with any reasonable club in our bag. We stand where our last considered stroke left our ball to lie considering when, how and where to attempt our next challenging shot. Unless you are Tiger Woods or some other professional you will probably hook or slice the ball a bit. You might end up in a sand trap or in the rough. Yet the well-planned terrain of a golf course will always keep you in reasonable safety from losing your way to the flag completely.
>
> Struggle-free Life is like a well-planned golf course. It keeps you playing in the fairway for most of the game. Even when you make mistakes that temporarily stall your progress, the agreement society makes to provide the means of return to your next starting point quickly after or around personal struggles is the compassionate action that keeps individual citizens and society as a whole inspired and ready for more.
>
> Rats! Your arc landed you in the sand trap! No problem. You've got a sand wedge for that. You are still keeping up with the rest of the players on your hole. A reasonable struggle may give us the opportunity to learn something complimentary to the path we have chosen to take toward our goals. In golf, that lesson is how to properly use your sand wedge by striking the sand directly behind the ball and not the ball itself. In life, you never know what that lesson may be. In Struggle-free Life you can be confident that whatever lessons bring to your personal education they will not destroy your motivation to continue.

When you take your joy and motivation with you through each struggle you are prepared to enjoy the finer moments of overcoming challenges with your growing competence. You not only feel progress being made but you are making progress in the way Capitalist society judges such things - your growing wealth and expressions of your joy of life under your ownership.

Money is not merely the ability to purchase goods or services. Money is the convenience to pick with greater detail and frequency your own perspective of joy becoming your personal view on Utopia. Over time, money is the means to own that perspective so that you can enjoy complementing it with other facets of your joy of life, improving it and sharing it with the people you choose.

On the golf course, it is the responsibility of the country club or municipal organization to keep unreasonable struggles that can cause your game harm outside the boundaries of the course itself. In our nation, the leaders and representatives we elect are the stewards of the Constitutional structure that keeps undo harm and unreasonable struggles away from our lives when they are forced upon us by other citizens, unfair rules, self-interested organizations misinterpreting the meaning of our rules or the manipulation of nations and people living outside our national borders projecting their intentions upon us.

In Utopian Capitalism philosophy, our understanding of money is updated for the twenty-first century so that it too may keep undo harm from our individual paths of life under our own direction. Money is no longer a mere component of economic structures within financial markets, banking and ownership. Money also moves into another rightful place within the architecture of our social structure itself. An intrinsic component of our right to a national environment that avoids the harm of flat or recessive progress personally and collectively.

As long as work and investment continues there will always be enough for everyone in the nation to achieve their own Struggle-Free Life with an individual perspective on Utopia. When government manages a monetary system achieving this for its citizens they are rewarded by unanimous agreement with debt-free monetary credit to fund faithful acts of value to society by Unanimous Consent.

At a time when our population is on track to expand toward half a billion people in our lifetimes we are expected more than ever to somehow improve our responsible behavior and meaningful outcomes in life. Struggle-free Life sets the foundation of our arcs of progress at the starting point so that we never again feel the unreasonable struggle of losing our financial growth and dropping through no fault of our own into the negative outcomes of dwindling and progressive cyclicality while the portion of society that have achieved wealth security continue to grow theirs through investments. Those harms of cyclical struggle are outside the boundary of a Utopian Capitalist society.

$40 Internet
$40 Telephone
$250 Healthcare
$200 Food
$30 Household Items
$500 Housing
$60 Transportation
$75 Utilities
$60 Clothing
* $500 Education Grant
* $~ Education Loans
10% Savings Bonds/Convertible Bills
$1381 PER MONTH

* As Needed

Figure 9Example of a Struggle-free Life Payment Amount

Struggle-free Life is achieved by determining the cost of meeting the personally responsible needs of physiology and ongoing safety of ourselves indicated within the lower two steps of Maslow's Hierarchy of Needs.

That amount, plus a small percentage on top to make a little progress as a good capitalist customer even if you find yourself long-term unemployed, will be paid to each American citizen monthly.

> **Consider this:** *With roughly 260 million adults in America the total amount of dollars to eliminate the poverty line in America by raising everyone above it is $4.4 trillion per year. That's a mere quarter of the current gross domestic product of America used to invigorate the American economy with each citizen's choice of where to purchase the essentials of a meaningful life*

we all agree we no longer will struggle to achieve.

Our society will make no earmark demands on us. Our government's sincerity - visible through active support of the environment we need to make responsible self-directed improvement as a population and a restatement of the philosophies of living we now champion as a nation for the good of the individual citizen - is all the guidance an improved and improving population needs to do the right thing with their Struggle-free Life perpetually.

Where does all this money come from? You may remember years ago that a group called the "99%" protested what they coined "fiat" currency. It turns out, currency that is as infinite as our future goals and plans for prosperity is the only sort of meaningful currency there is.

Any form of wealth supported by a value other than a nation's faith and credit within, among and for itself is an investment - unsuitable for long-term stability. When you become aware of Infinite Currency supported by secular faith in the people that grow their wealth through work, appreciation and verifiable credit you realize it is a truth worthy of respect and remembrance.

Don't take my word for it. Investigate the philosophy and think about the suggestions for yourself. Consider the positive societal perspectives that Utopian Capitalism parallels in its intention and the benefits to individuals in society its structure can achieve when those intentions are coupled with the improving and more joyful lives that result to carry them forward along a responsible collection of paths of personal artistry of life with greater inspiration and long-term momentum.

SECTION IV
Swimming in the
Wealth Pool

Two Lives Colorful
We Hold All Things Wonderful
Wait Refundable

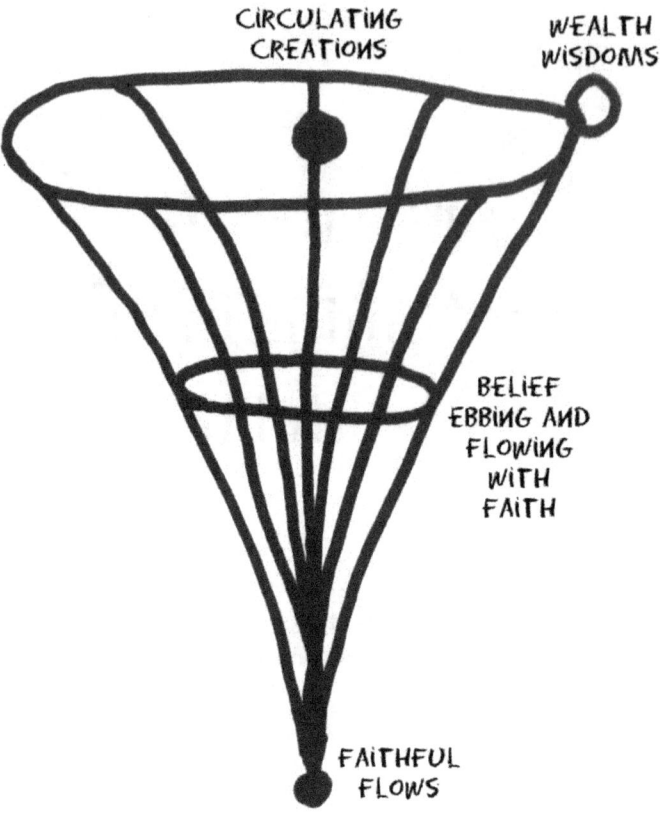

Figure 10Spring of Renewal. This geometry represents an opening of new perspectives for civil life and liberty in pursuit of happiness. Over time, delegated frameworks of complementary support create stairways of certain traversal shaping the spring into a pyramid.

CHAPTER 7
Facet One: Faithful Flows

INFINITE CURRENCY

UTOPIA IS MORE MONEY THAN ANYONE CAN APPRECIATE.

Currency is, and should always be, infinite in order to provide a future environment for billions of Americans that keeps the value of their work as close to consistent as possible. The primary means of supporting faith from, toward and among all citizens is using Infinite Currency to provide everyone with a Struggle-free Life. Once this compassionate action overcomes our collective national struggle there are many other challenges for our nation to focus upon.

As long as we maintain a growing population, appreciable assets and Faithful Expenditures the concept of currency as an infinite abundance is the only sound concept to describe the availability of our faithful money supply. Just as everything else government stewards within our domestic boundaries, how we view our currency is completely within our society's control. Infinite Currency by Unanimous Consent is the parallel complement to investment appreciation that introduces brand new currency into our wealth pool.

When currency is infinite the faith you have in the people who earn and spend it and the credit you give to the government and organizations that manage it with integrity are the primary means of stability for that currency.

Convertible Currency

A potential for pure faith involvement from citizen back to society exists in the form of Convertible Notes. Currency earmarked for use by employers to pay for work with a redemption period is a compromise with the notion of investment-backed currency that functions more like a savings bond. People receiving convertible notes may use them at face value or hold them past the redemption date to receive an appreciated return from their money. The faithfulness of what might be used as a commemorative currency is based upon the Unanimous Consent of one citizen and their faith in the society that chooses to issue them brand new currency for it.

When paid out as part of the savings portion of a Struggle-free Life payment convertible currency becomes a gauge by which savings patterns of the population can be analyzed with data from redemption points.

RECYCLED CURRENCY

Understanding the movement of currency within our wealth pool is a meaningful component of understanding what our society does with its faith. Understandings by statistical analysis and localized movement of the ebb and flow of money passing in circles through our economic cycle is critical to understanding the environments which inspire citizens to convert their faith into their wealth as lasting Joys of Life.

RETIRED CURRENCY

You can't take it with you – but you can share it! As we accrue our monetary faith in savings throughout our lives we should consider an important fact about faith. Faith cannot be shared. Faith is a personal experience whether it is found in a church, in a song, in a smile or in the money we save from the work we did because our employers had faith in us to achieve it and proved it by paying us in our nationally-recognized faith – money. Faith is amassed from all angles around a source of faith. When we have enough faith in our secure future accrued within a savings account the next step to achieving something with it is to risk some of it on our Joys of Life.

Joys of Life are the paths we take to achieve an expression of our love that we may own, maintain and share with the people we choose. When we die we can't pass on our faith by passing on a stack of money. We can inspire faith, however, by passing on a home, an investment, an art collection or even a shoebox full of stocks and bonds. Whatever our Joys of Life are they remain for whomever we leave them to upon our passing. Our currency savings will retire. The notion of impressing the living with as much as could be saved in a bank while living a miserly life is a detriment to the ability to find and hold onto the things we create and obtain contributing to a richer, more enjoyable world for us all. With the exception of a reasonable threshold of monetary assets, the currency we accrue during our life will be retired from the wealth pool at our death to maintain a natural ebb and flow. If you really love that money and want to pass it on make sure you do it while you are still alive.

CHAPTER 8
Facet Two: Circulating Creations

CORPORATE APPRENTICESHIPS

LOVE IS A KEEN AUTEUR IN WHICHEVER POOL IT SWIMS.

Modular Managed Corporations

Modular Managed Corporations are architected with an inner complement of fundamental corporate roles staffed to share and multiple opportunities of attached leadership, management and employee roles connected by patent-able business methods specific to the industry allowing shared community resources of fundamental concern (CFO, Marketing, Branding, CIO, etc) to be funded easily by an external source while empowering entrepreneurs to achieve full working corporations with minimal cost.

I suggest these corporate structures usher in the age of corporate apprenticeships in tune with the sharing economy. Parent companies with a platform product such as an engine, a hardware device, a sound mechanism, a visual display or any other item built for continued customization prior to offering in the consumer market will benefit. Craftsmen attach themselves and their mission-focused employees in support of the platform invention akin to miners staking claims for gold in California.

Benefits of this geometry include the ability to wind down individual held structures with no negative impact to the attached ongoing concerns and ease of detachment for held modules that seek to create their own senior management-level complements as they mature. This corporate structure can facilitate ease of ownership for apprentices within a platformed product incubator utilizing a shared, fundamental corporate structure for entrepreneurs. Costs for scale are mitigated up to the limit of what the fundamental product owner can operate making the operating costs of the fundamental structure a reasonable burden for the platform incubator to bear.

This corporate structure also makes sponsorship of platform incubators possible. Independent professional services groups catering to an industry and seeking a share of the growth potential can easily gift themselves into the fundamental structure when the incubator's ownership seeks to minimize their costs or involvement. Even spin-offs and partnerships can find value in the modularity for the clear separation of its business focus from parent or partner organizations.

When viewed from the perspective of an idea proving ground this architecture allows growth of the successful entrepreneurships to easily maintain as lesser successes detach with the result becoming business units of a mature corporation no longer in need of platform incubation benefits.

Finally, in nation's supporting long-term master-planning of their progress this corporate architecture makes it easy to fund by grant, angel or other investments the specific improvements presented by the platform as well as all apprentice entrepreneurs involved in role modeling its value to the consumer and external craftsmen.

Cascading Manufacturing System

A Cascading Manufacturing System takes into account the artistry of other seller-side contributors within a product sale for the sake of expanded options and opportunities of product customization for a consumer to enjoy.

> **Consider this:** *A manufacturer of electric automotive engines creates a new Modular Managed Corporation to be a platform incubator for a new line of engines built for home and garden usage. Artists of an engineering kind attach to the incubator adding their skill to development of products benefitting from an electric engine. In doing so, patterns and layers emerge*

defining the ways in which the manufacturing process down to the consumer can be layered for customizations. These are noted by the Modular Managed Corporation's officer who does so.

Once the incubator has run its course the knowledge of patterns and layers of creation around the engine is used to transition or spin-off the organization into a Cascading Manufacturing System. Anyone interested in the artistry of business is now included – an inversion of the platform incubator's concept surrounding a prominent kind of artistic creation. In this example, consider that a modular lawnmower has been invented. Opening the manufacturing process at key points to include those wishing to supply housings made up of fiberglass, aluminum, structured ceramic or high-end mahogany becomes possible. Those external businesses are shipped the engines for attachment to their housings.

At that point, the cascading items such as wheels, blades, vacuum bags and other attachments are introduced from a further level of external organization and individuals. Graphic artists working at the point of sale or independently with the consumer utilize templates to create unique customizations by computer uploaded into the process for hand-off to painters or mechanized finishing processes.

INSPIRATION ENVIRONMENTS

Domestic Environments

While considering the unemployment problems the Obama Administration dealt with on a perfect statistical arc I was caught by a notion of national unemployment as the only mode of unemployment states have ever faced. The fact that the United States tends to face economic conditions together has been unquestioned as a norm. Yet when you consider that our fifty states reflect unique personalities of common interest just as nations are to the world it becomes nothing but peculiar that our states suffer depressive cycles as a group even as the world economy does not. In fact, the world economy has never succumbed to a collective depression as far as we know – only the developed nations have done so.

I suggest unemployment has, until recently, been an unattended lever of harm avoidance to our population. Perhaps shortsightedly seen as a means to a federal-level solution replacing war as a regular good that states alone are unequipped to provide when it creates a level of despair that is manageable. Reporting job statistics at the short end (5% unemployment vs. 95% employment) is somewhat a pessimistic situation to begin with. Expectations that negativity should ripple throughout our system without stopping at the feet of any of the more powerful state economies adds to a necessary suspension of disbelief in our sustainability as a collective economic leadership on Earth.

> **Consider this:** *If there were only one billion people in the world would that be enough to make all the money we need to be happy? What if those people all lived in America? Could we sustain a single economic territory without outside involvement given the amount of natural resources we are gifted with and the inspired supports of happiness we provide as we seek it?*
>
> *Assuming for a moment that the United States could not stabilize its economy without foreign trade and investment I suggest we develop a plan to do so. In doing so, I suggest we will find the awareness guiding us to long-term structures of stability for the world economy as well.*
>
> *I suggest monetary unions alone cannot endure unless they exist as social unions of plural monetary means achieving balance through time with understandings of national personality, perspective and planning and the secular faiths of each domestic population involved.*

Unemployment is only an indicator of who wants to work and cannot find it. To have focused on unemployment statistics with intentional association of meaning to the economic condition of America on the whole has kept concern for solely domestic economic sustainability from being considered. I suggest that sustainability over time is not as much a priority for our nation as sustainability within our domestic territory at any time.

Now that we have a blueprint for improvement to reflect upon in the run-up to future unemployment issues with the "Obama Arc" we can fix our gaze upon the flexible strength of our economic system. I suggest the components are most easily understood, at first, by their correlation to our Wealth Pool. Understanding our Wealth Pool will set the stage for understanding our economic and social personality as a nation and our personality's contribution to the sustainable happiness of the world.

Domestic Inspirations

As citizens, once there is a strong foundation upon which to be reasonably certain we can risk some of our savings on an expression of ourselves by purchase or creation we look for an inspiration to help us achieve it. Struggle-free Life gives all of us the ability to remain calm and wait for the inspiration to achieve our best lives in our own best way as long as it does no harm to any other citizen's path to their Joy of Life. Direct inspirations such as art classes, workshops, Modular Managed Corporation platform incubators and all of the entrepreneurial or domestically comforting projects we can think up will benefit from an environment of apprenticeship renaissance.

International Motivation to Inspire Domestically

As agreements between countries, treaties and United Nations mandates begin to create a long-term world master-planning direction there ought to be a way to provide incentive for countries who decide to support it. Master Planning Multipliers placed onto work and investment specifics that contribute to our world's progress do just that.

If space travel and habitation of the moon is a goal then a 2 or 3 multiplier next to aerospace or deep space careers and investment choices will boost a nation's overall value if it focuses effort in those areas. If not, no big deal. It's a giveaway for team players. Nations focused on domestic issues can always ignore world directions while they stabilize and invigorate their own part of our Earth contributing to their domestic awareness.

For nations that contribute in other ways to a shared vision of a more wonderful Earth, such as pollution reduction treaties, common rights and liberties, bans on violent behaviors and outcomes, multipliers or other financial value incentives that add value to national wealth from the international perspective to make those nations' currencies stronger in the international marketplace will be a fair and transparent way to reward good behavior to replace the concept of sanctioning bad behavior. All this aids creation of a better metaphor for progress with integrity in the capitalist way.

JOYS OF LIFE

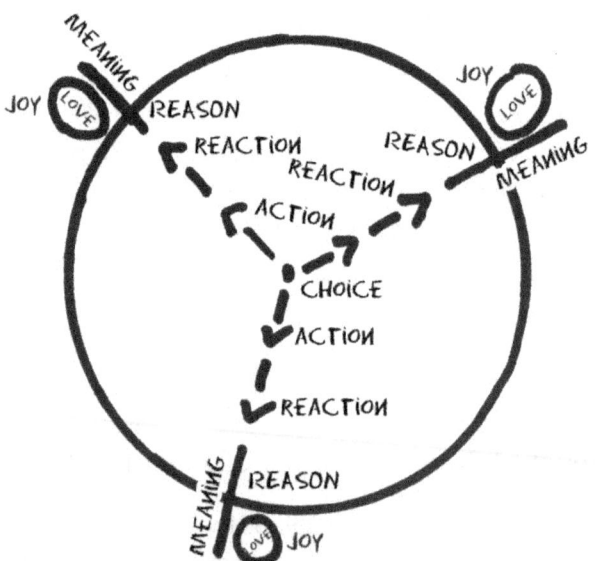

JOY SPHERES ROUNDING THE EARTH

I suggest understanding more fully the concept of sharing our Joys of Life with others will give way to new awareness of what we can achieve from our inspired works and collaborative works with others. For instance, families that have come to enjoy their time on their grandparent's farm who may have considered dividing up the land after their grandparents pass away may now consider a more collaborative option. Creation of a familial corporate structure allowing shares of willable Joys of Life to be divided among the heirs so that property and investment remain whole for the future allow individuals to liquidate their share to siblings and others without diminishing the value of the inheritance fully intact.

Helping each other up the ladder of financial flexibility in order to create some thing or reflect some piece of our lives that share our joy of living will become a value to our local environs. As such, it makes sense that innovations to existing means of gaining credit to achieve them faster will spring up. As existing banks move their focus to lending in the six figures credit unions of neighbors getting together with small amounts of savings to invest will find a financial services modular managed platform supported by a savings and loan business process and the professional corporate staffing helpful in organizing and maintaining a neighborhood lending organization. Small gardens, parks, playgrounds and many other meaningful projects can be undertaken, and underwritten with credit from their neighbors, close to home by those who love doing so in order to pass on their Joy of Life to the future in ways that existing bank loan officers cannot appreciate.

CHAPTER 9
Facet Three: Wealth Wisdoms

FOREIGN WEALTHS

Commercial Exchange Rates

As methods of control and limitation give way to inspired means of promoting commerce it makes sense to do away with tariffs in order to establish an ongoing support of foreign interests establishing wealth in America.

> **Consider this:** *Imagine a first world nation intending to support its industries with profit from American satellite companies. Our Commerce Secretary has experience in the nation and feels they are likely to abuse our prosperity somewhat by making and taking their profits back to their own country. In such a situation, manipulation of a Commercial Exchange Rate going out to that nation's currency from our own makes sense.*

Commercial Exchange Rates determined and indicated by a domestic organization of integrity will provide a lever with which we can reward those companies keeping their dollar earnings circulating in America. If they choose to sell their widgets and walk away without improving our economy with money multipliers they face a degradation of the normal exchange rate as a backend penalty. If they stay in America, reinvest their earnings and improve our economy they maintain the value of their earnings and prosper as an American company with foreign involvement.

The benefits of this means of inspiring foreign business growth in America are:

1. No tariffs are passed on the back of products by default. If a company decides to pad their prices in anticipation of leaving the country with their money they place that indication on their products themselves.
2. Simplification of the documentation required to enter the American market from abroad. Less hassle, more efficient movement of goods.
3. U.S. Customs will focus less on taxation limitations and do more to streamline foreign involvement in our product markets as well as innovated controls upon unregistered floods of foreign competitor goods that would harm our foreign wealth investors. In this way, they set the stage for an integrated system of national Customs standards benefiting faith from the corporate perspective as it turns into trust.
4. Comparison of the relative treatment of each nation's commercial interest in America can be easily calculated as a means for foreign nations to understand their actual standing in our eyes. Such an openness in our judgments and awareness of our economic inputs and outputs is a strong role model for other nations to follow.
5. No tariffs up front means greater selection of more products entering our nation and more investment capital to hire larger American staff to sell them.
6. Our government can regulate commercial issues in currency separate from civilian currency conversion. From a State Department perspective, this sends a better message of civilian friendliness than singular, nondirectional currency exchange rate manipulation.
7. Fosters the awareness that the single standard for monetary value in the world is the one your country places upon all others with its own.
8. Penalizes poor corporate actors while leaving our true foreign investors unharmed by regulation just as a domestic entity should be.
9. Sets a responsible example for world governments to follow contributing to successful Faith Management.
10. When role modeled to other nations this method allows American companies to expand more economically into foreign nations. As a leader of industry on Earth, this allows us to "hand-me-down" the structures of our industries for foreign national master plans seeking compliments to their national personality and stair steps assisting our economic allies while building our strength as a corporate investment nation abroad in ways supportive of their future rather than direct it – with our wisdom proven in business. U.S. energy companies have learned to do this with energy production facilities as environmental

standards have risen. Other industries will learn to do it their own way too. Perhaps even seeding international efforts with older generations of technology and infrastructure more easily learned and utilized for the times and places of their expansions or which support shifts of production center for former generation products deemed innovations or complements in other nations.

Everything in every way in its own time as economies choose. Using this standard for inspiring onshore profits to stay onshore in conjunction with a reasonable standard of using the International Value Markets reports to automatically calculate a default exchange rate make rate control by our government or a third-party integrity akin to the Federal Reserve a faithful potential Americans can trust.

DOMESTIC WEALTH

Supporting the appreciation, renewal and periodic replacement of our domestic wealth as owned by citizens and immigrants maintains this largest segment of the total wealth pool of our nation. As we grow to understand more fully the character, geometry and value of our domestic wealth in detail it will be motivated by a reflection of the international master planning multipliers innovated for domestic use and applied to citizens and corporations achieving Joys of Life with permanence of inheritable quality in line with our national way forward.

SHARED WEALTH

Details of our society's infrastructure such as our transportation systems, our communications networks and our terraforming achievements will be understood more thoroughly as we move forward with the Wealth Pool in mind. Shared Wealth of our nation will be an understanding of domestic pride, awareness and involvement with our pasts and our collective futures. Learning from the identified balance of domestic, foreign and shared wealth in our society will allow us to more effectively describe our national personality and express it through shared wealth supporting economic vitality.

ABOUT THE AUTHOR

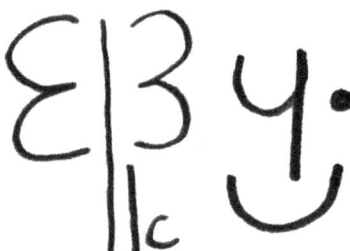

Ewan Lillicii is an exceptional philosopher from La Grange, Larkspur, and Las Vegas. This book of love was written in Las Vegas, Los Angeles, Weimar, La Grange, Oakland, Roseville, Sacramento, Stanislaus Forest, Temple, Boston, Winthrop and all rest stops on the road in between. Thanks Andrew I, Carrie Shakespeare, Charlie, Christian, Christine, Derrick, Emilio, Emily, Esmeralda, Ewan Dei, Hillary, Leonardo, Lili, Madonna, Marc, Mark, Native Americans, Question Mark, Martin, Martin, Melania, Merovich, Ericka, Paris, Paris, Q.T., Ray, Sarah, Sarah, Shari Shakespeare, Teal, William, Mom, family and friends for your support.

Super Silly Charm
Instinctually No Harm
Fires The Alarmed

"Paddle me across the sea, Paddlebee."